TH

WALKING THE JURA HIGH ROUTE
Kev Reynolds .... *Page 3*

WINTER SKI TRAVERSES
R. Brian Evans .... *Page 121*

CICERONE PRESS
MILNTHORPE, CUMBRIA, ENGLAND

Cicerone Press,
2 Police Square,
Milnthorpe,
Cumbria
England

ISBN 1-85284-009-2

ACKNOWLEDGEMENTS

My thanks to Franz Blum at the Swiss National Tourist
Office in London, and to many other members of the
staff of the Tourist Offices in the Jura for their assistance.
To Lisbeth and Erich Spielmann whose instant warmth
and generosity made my day when luck was fading. To
Ursula Flückiger for her hospitality, friendship and
readiness to help on several occasions. And to Nigel Fry
who walked the High Route with me and shared my
eagerness for each 'Sinalco stop' along the way.

I am grateful, too, to Brian Evans who was already
working on a winter guide to the Jura when the High
Route was first mooted, and who readily agreed to a
combined effort with this guidebook. Thanks.

Kev Reynolds

Thanks, Kev for allowing me to share your book. Special
thanks to my companions - we've had some great days
and unusual lodgings. To Albert Riding and Gladys
Sellers, both septegenarians with an undiminished sense
of adventure. To sturdy trailbreakers John Riding and
Raif Evans. To cheerful novices Dave and Corinne
Murray who didn't know what they were letting themselves in for. To Swiss friend Gunter Zeh who must have
wondered if he should have stayed at home. And last but
by no means least to my ever supportive wife Aileen.

Brian Evans

THE JURA

Walking the Jura High Route
Kev Reynolds

Photos by the author

*Front Cover Top: At the edge of the Creux du Van.
Photo: Kev Reynolds*

*Front Cover Bottom: Above the Col de la Faucille on the Traverse of
the Crêtes. Photo: Brian Evans*

*Back Cover: Mont Blanc and the Chamonix Aiguilles from Colomby de
Gex. Photo: Brian Evans.*

The large open spaces of the Val de Joux, between Mont Tendre and Col de Marchairuz.

CONTENTS

Introduction   7
The Jura High Route   9
Getting There - And Back Again 12
Accommodation 13
Notes for Walkers 14
Recommended Maps 16
Practical Information 19
Using this Guide 20

Stage 1:   Dielsdorf to Brugg. 23
Stage 2:   Brugg to Staffelegg 32
Stage 3:   Staffelegg to Hauenstein 38
Stage 4:   Hauenstein to Balsthal 44
Stage 5:   Balsthal to Weissenstein 53
Stage 6:   Weissenstein to Frinvillier 58
Stage 7:   Frinvillier to Chasseral 63
Stage 8:   Chasseral to Neuchâtel 68
Stage 9:   Neuchâtel to Le Soliat 73
Stage 10:   Le Soliat to Sainte-Croix 81
Stage 11:   Sainte-Croix to Vallorbe 87
Stage 12:   Vallorbe to Col du Marchairuz 92
Stage 13:   Col du Marchairuz to St. Cergue 100
Stage 14:   St. Cergue to Borex 105

Summary Table of Route and Timings for the Jura Höhenweg 111
Principal Alternative Routes of the JHR 113
Feeder Routes 116
Useful Addresses 118

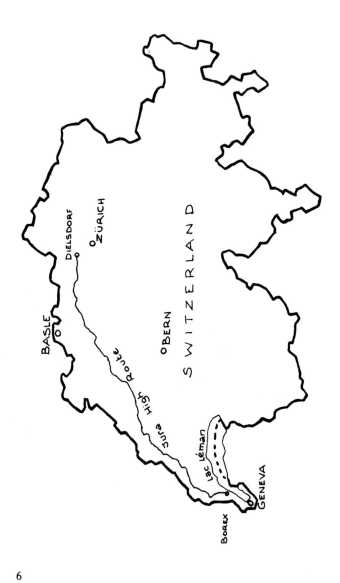

ZÜRICH

DIELSDORF

BASLE

Route

High

Jura

O BERN

S W I T Z E R L A N D

Lac Léman

GENEVA

BOREX

INTRODUCTION

Day six...a wet day. Rain from mid-morning sweeping in gusts from the unseen south-west. Struggling against the wind over open pastures knee deep in sopping grass... Lunch in a deserted hut behind which cattle sheltered from the weather. Continuing, we came suddenly to an opening in the clouds...the rain stopped...the wind dropped, and as we wandered over a bluff all the world fell at our feet and we looked far out to the south and the east, out beyond the great flat plain of rich agricultural land to a distant horizon of dreams. There, with clouds below and clouds above, sandwiched by layers of vapour, hung the big Oberland peaks: Eiger, Mönch and Jungfrau in a long line of powder-white waves. Among those waves were the Finsteraarhorn, Breithorn, Blümlisalp and Doldenhorn, each one trapped for a moment in time among the clouds. A moment of magic...

Other days when the sun beat down from a sky stretched taut from one horizon to another while we strode along green crests, broad with pastures, rich in wild flowers and with hawks wheeling on high, measuring our pace with their shadows... The clatter of cowbells; the seething of summer-warm grasses...a red-roofed village tucked neatly in a fold of valley. And peace all around...

Evening on the rim of the Creux du Van...a huge limestone cirque plunging from the pathway to forests seen like a mattress of moss three hundred metres and more below. In the depths mist played a game of hide and seek. Teased by a restless wind, that mist was plucked to reveal jigsaw snatches of white cliff, green forest and river...then all was closed again from us. A soft and pure light played on tomorrow's hills...galleon sails of cumulus drifted across the high plateau of Le Bied...a brocken spectre cast into the mist...the fragrance of wood-smoke from a nearby farm...

Treasures from the Jura.

*   *   *

It could be said that the Jura are Switzerland's unknown mountains. Unlike their dramatic neighbours, the Alps, and considerably lower in altitude, (their highest Swiss summit, Mont Tendre, is 1,679m) they long ago traded their glaciers and permanent fields of snow in favour of pastureland and forest. Now they run in parallel crests of green hill and scooped valley in a long arc down the western rim of the country to form a natural frontier with France. Indeed, the Jura belongs as much to France as it does to Switzerland, and long after the white cross has ceased to fly over isolated farms, the Jura continues as a ridge of limestone above French valleys and French villages with Mont Blanc saluting from afar.

This great rectangle of hills contains a lush series of landscapes; friendly, welcoming, pastoral. There are wild flowers in abundance, rich meadows, dense forests, glorious beechwoods. And views off to the Alps, way beyond the levels of the Mittelland.

Across these hills there's a long-distance walking route that explores the very best of the Swiss Jura; the *Jurahöhenweg* to German-speaking Swiss, *Chemin des Crêtes du Jura* in French. To English speaking hill walkers it is the Jura High Route.

The Jura High Route (JHR) is 299 kilometres long, stretching from Dielsdorf, outside Zürich, to Borex, a small village to the north of Geneva. Along the way it passes over the highest summits of the Swiss Jura. (Mont Tendre, La Dôle, Chasseral, each over 1,600 metres.) It traverses meadowland and forest and visits isolated farms, secluded villages locked in a world all their own, historic small towns, ruined castles. There are stretches of riverside walking, and belvedere paths that trace the very crest of the ridge with huge views to embrace an ever-varied panorama. There are time-moulded pastures, soft underfoot, and limestone terraces smoothed by wind and rain and ice-sheets that once bore down from the Alps. For much of the route the hills and their valleys are virtually empty of people. There's an aura of solitude that can rarely be experienced among the higher Alps where the paths are too often crowded.

Here in the Jura it is possible to take a walk in the sky undisturbed by the crowds.

The Jura and its High Route offer an unhurried sense of calm, a pedestrian adventure in a world of green.

* * *

The Jura High Route

Little-known to visitors from Britain though it may be, the JHR presents a splendid challenge to those who enjoy a long walk through an unspoilt, largely pastoral, landscape. A walk across Switzerland that can be achieved inside a fortnight's holiday, it travels not only the length of the Swiss Jura, but also crosses the language divide from German to French-speaking cantons - a divide that is as evident in architecture and culture as it is linguistic.

It begins in a modest, pleasing agricultural landscape halfway between the commercial whirl of Zürich and the green borders of Germany. Dielsdorf slumbers below a hill of fruit and forest in a back-country farmland. It's a gentle beginning, but there are lovely views and an aura of tranquility as the path climbs up through the glorious little hilltop village of Regensberg and onto the limestone crest of Lägeren where flowers cluster in crevices beside the path and all the world lies spread below.

There are the charming old towns of Baden and Brugg - the first built on a curve of the Limmat river, the second on the Aare - and then it's back to the hills and forest again. Back to pastures lined with cherry trees, with solitary farms hugging folds of meadowland, and villages that few tourists ever see, but that are delightful and unspoilt and as picturesque as any that regularly appear on calendars, chocolate boxes and postcards.

The hills grow in stature as the High Route works its way south-westwards, and suddenly promontories display huge panoramas - bigger and broader than you'll find from many much higher mountains where distances are bewildered by intervening peaks. Here the ranges roll away in mellow waves, their slopes patterned by stripes of yellow and gold and half a dozen shades of green, with big rivers winding through the valleys, spawned among glaciers and snowfields of peaks that hang upon the distant horizon.

At the end of the fifth day the walker comes to a hint of the possibilities of winter enjoyment of the Jura. The Weissenstein (1,284m) above Solothurn has its mechanical aids for the ski-buff, but as Brian Evans points out elsewhere in this book, the Jura is a wonderland for the cross-country skier, and up here it is the touring skier, rather than the downhill enthusiast, who will gain most in winter, while in summer the meadow slopes are bright with flowers and loud with the clatter of cowbells.

West of the Weissenstein the southern slopes are scooped into bowls of pasture, with farms that look out over the great expanse of the Mittelland, while to the north one ridge sweeps off to another, and then another and yet more until the corrugations of successive Jura hills fade blue and mysterious against the sky. France lies among those ridges, and its influence is gradually felt even here in Switzerland as the dominant language is no longer German, but French, and the architecture of one or two villages has more than a hint of Gallic expression. Here the route becomes rather less a *Höhenweg* and more a *Chemin des Crêtes* as it climbs up to the viewpoint of Chasseral (1,607m), overlooking the lakes of Biel and Neuchâtel; seas of blue glinting in the sunlight rather than seas of green.

From Chasseral the JHR offers an alternative with an option to avoid dropping into Neuchâtel by skirting along a secondary ridge to Vue des Alpes, then over Tête de Ran and Mont Racine to Noraigue. The standard route, which visits Neuchâtel, then runs along the edge of vineyards to enter the cool dark narrows of the Gorges de l'Areuse and up a steep forest climb to Le Soliat on the rim of the spectacular limestone cirque, the Creux du Van. Here both routes join once more to continue heading south-westward, over the lofty point of Le Chasseron (1,607m) and down among yet more flower meadows where in winter skiers swoop in flurries of powder snow to the neat village of Sainte-Croix, home of the musical box industry.

Suddenly the Jura seems to have been 'discovered', for there are shops specifically geared to the tourist industry - so rare along this route that has thus far given every impression of being through an unknown country.

Leaving Sainte-Croix the High Route takes it easy for half a morning, wandering through a gentle slope of broad meadowland with France only a field or two away, before a sharp haul leads onto the crest of the ridge once more at Le Suchet (1,588m) and then descends on the south side to Vallorbe, a surprise of a village with an international railway station and a delightfully picturesque heart where the River Orbe paints its influence on waterside buildings. But after Vallorbe the route heads into forest and across a moorland-like pastoral land until the climb to the highest point of the Swiss Jura, Mont Tendre (1,679m). Not a great summit, but a point on a limestone and grass ridge overlooking the much-loved Vallée de Joux to the west, and a sweep of farmland to the east leading to Lac Léman (the Lake of Geneva). And out there, beyond the farmlands, beyond the great lake, soar the snowpeaks of the Alps.

Perhaps the walk from Mont Tendre over Grand Cunay to Col du Marchairuz is among the very best of the Jura High Route. Given the blessings of a clear sky and warm sunshine, the fold of hills and valleys, the pattern of distant forest, the brilliance of limestone-loving plants at your feet and the views that stretch off to vast distances devoid of towns or cities or even villages, will remain one of the highlights of the walk. Then beyond the col the path heads from one seemingly lost farm to another on an easy undulating course as far as Saint Cergue, another trim village that comes alive under a mantle of winter snow. La Dôle rises above the village; the final climb, the last summit of a long walk. It's not much of a summit since it has been adorned with rather too much of man's technological marvels - important, perhaps, for modern communications and to aid airport safety, but an eyesore to long-distance walkers attuned to uncluttered hills. But the views are vast indeed, and eyes will be drawn to far-off snow and ice before the long descent takes you south-eastwards off the Jura heights and down to a sudden level agricultural land and a quiet lane that goes direct to Borex, in whose village centre beside a gushing water trough the 299 kilometres of the Jura High Route officially end. Not far off spreads the lake of Geneva. Beyond that rise the Dents du Midi and Mont Blanc - challenges for another year.

*   *   *

On a practical level, the route is waymarked throughout its length either by conspicuous use of diamond-shaped plates fixed to trees, buildings or fence-posts, or by paint flashes on rocks. The JHR colouring for these waymarks is red and yellow, while on the ubiquitous yellow signposts that appear in villages and towns and at strategic crosstracks in the hills, the JHR continuation has a triangular section of the finger-plate painted red. In common with other regions of Switzerland, certain of these signposts contain an indication, not of distance in terms of kilometres, but of the amount of walking time required to reach those places named - Std (*Stunden*, which is German for hours) or h. (*heures*) and min. In addition, occasional markers will be found indicating *Höhenweg* (in German-speaking areas) or *Chemin des Crêtes* (in French-speaking cantons). The frequency with which these waymarks occur changes from canton to canton, but rarely will any route-finding difficulty arise as the footpaths and tracks are almost always clear, except when crossing uncut meadowlands, in which case there will be sufficient direction indicators nearby.

The route described in this guidebook is the main JHR which will take about fourteen days of travel at around 6 hours of walking time per day, plus rest stops. Times quoted are based on those given on signposts along the route. Clearly these can only be estimations based on an average gained over specific sections, and each individual walker

11

will probably find it necessary to make some adjustments to these times when forweard planning a day's journey. But whilst the end of each day's stage will be determined by the availability of accommodation, do not be tempted to 'race' the times quoted. They are there for guidance only, not as a challenge! Wander the Jura at a relaxed and comfortable pace that will enable you to absorb the countryside through which you walk.

There are alternative stages and linking routes that join the main JHR from neighbouring regions, for example from Dornach (Basle), from Rheinfelden or Liestal, and brief details of these sections are given at the conclusion of the main route description. But it is, perhaps, more satisfactory to complete the full route from Dielsdorf to Borex (Zürich to Geneva), as described.

Getting There - And Back Again

Excellent public transport links exist between the U.K. and Switzerland, and within Switzerland the superb rail and Postbus services ensure that almost any part of the country is within easy reach, even without private means of transport.

For those who prefer air travel, several daily flights are available throughout the summer from British airports to Zürich, Basle and Geneva.

Swissair flights operate in conjunction with British Airways from London (Heathrow), Manchester and Dublin. Air services from North America fly to Geneva and/or Zürich from Boston, Chicago, Los Angeles, Montreal and New York. Those airlines that maintain a service across the Atlantic are Swissair, Trans World Airlines and Air Canada.

Zürich is the most convenient airport for visitors setting out on the Jura High Route, but both Basle and Geneva are equally well placed for travels in other regions of these mountains.

By rail it is feasible to board a train at London's Victoria station at lunch-time on Saturday, and be setting out on the walk from Dielsdorf at breakfast-time on Sunday having slept overnight on the journey in a couchette. Routes between London and Basle vary, but there is only one main-line routing between Basle and Zürich. Change at Zürich for Oberglatt (the Schaffhausen line), and at Oberglatt a branch line will deliver you in about seven minutes to Dielsdorf for the start of the JHR.

At the end of the walk there is an infrequent Postbus service from Borex to Nyon, which has main-line connections with Geneva; or alternatively, take the north-bound train from Nyon to Lausanne to

The Youth Hostel at Brugg, a convenient overnight stop at the end of Stage One.

pick up the Paris connection (via Vallorbe). The super-fast TGV takes this route to Paris, and will practically halve travelling time to the French capital.

Accommodation

Because of the scarcity of available water supplies en route (the Jura is a limestone range) wild camping is not really practicable. There are few official campsites anywhere near the route, so it is hardly worth carrying a tent. (A sentence written after bitter experience!)

However, there is little shortage of gasthof or hotel accommodation, and there are a few farms that offer a somewhat basic standard of overnight lodging, i.e. *Touristenlager* or *dortoir* (communal dormitories). Although there are several S.A.C. (Swiss Alpine Club) huts along the route, unlike those found in the high mountain regions of the Alps, they are open only at weekends, or when members have booked during the week, so they cannot be relied upon. At present there are several Youth Hostels offering dormitory accommodation that can conveniently be used by YHA members. Details are given

13

where they occur, but check the International Handbook (or the Swiss Youth Hostel Guide) for up-to-date information. (It is worth taking out membership in advance of travelling to Switzerland as the cost is considerably more expensive when joining in an overseas country - see the Appendix for YHA address.)

It is, perhaps, worth mentioning that the price of accommodation for this route need not be frighteningly high. By using an assortment of lodgings, the total cost does not become exorbitant, no matter what you might deduce from study of normal Swiss hotel price lists. In many cases the cost of an overnight in a Jura hotel will be less than at a similar standard of hotel in Britain.

Accommodation information is given with regard to each day's stage of the walk where it occurs, but for specific up-to-date lists of hotels, gasthofs etc. contact the Swiss National Tourist Office. (Address is given in the Appendix.)

Notes for Walkers
Walking the Jura is an experience all its own. It is unlike wandering among the high Alps. It is quite different to rambling in a lowland region and has few comparisons in Britain. Sometimes the route climbs through pine forest. Sometimes it leads across a rolling green ridge at 1,500 metres, or along a narrow limestone trail high above a valley, yet with beech trees growing along it. On occasion the route is almost moorland in quality. Sometimes it follows a deserted country lane, or winds through a village. On the first day's stage it visits two towns and actually goes along a railway platform that is waymarked! More often than not it follows a lonely - yet lovely - course over high pastures among acres of wild flowers and with birds singing overhead. Always it is interesting. Invariably it is scenically delightful.

Although it is neither a lowland walk nor a high mountain trek, there is something of both about it. As a consequence one should think carefully about the type of clothing and equipment to choose. The period in which to tackle the JHR is summer to autumn (mid-June to October inclusive). However, should the weather turn inhospitable (and even in July this is possible) the walker will find that an exposed hilltop at 1,500 or 1,600 metres can be quite cold, so warm, windproof outer clothing will be an important item of equipment, as will waterproof cagoule and overtrousers. Goretex-type 'breathable' material is so widely available now that weatherproof gear made from this will provide an outer cover that is both wind and water-resistant.

For most summer walking shorts and a light shirt will be adequate, and a hat with a brim will help to protect the head and neck from the effects of too much sun. A high-factor suncream should also be taken as a protection for skin exposed to the strong ultra-violet light of the mountains.

Boots are the walker's most important item of equipment. Light, comfortable and with a good vibram-type sole to provide adequate grip on limestone paths and steep grass slopes, are essential. In addition, a pair of trainers or sandals should be carried in the rucksack for evening wear in hotels or hostels.

The choice of rucksack is also important since it is your daily support system and the one item, next to your boots, that must fit most comfortably of all to your body. If it doesn't, you will know about it - and have reason to curse it - for every one of the 299 kilometres of the High Route! Do not be tempted to carry too much in it. After all, this is not so much a backpacking trip as a long series of linked day walks. You will not need to carry a tent, nor a sleeping bag nor cooking equipment, nor food for more than a day. All that is needed in addition to the above mentioned items is a change of clothing, including a warm pullover, toilet items, food for lunch, maps, whistle, compass, first aid kit, mending kit, torch and water bottle of at least 1 litre capacity. A supply of plastic bags can be very useful for containing clothing within the rucksack in the event of wet weather, and also to store recently-laundered spare clothes in prior to getting them dry.

The availability of fresh water supplies is a point worth noting. Unlike many mountain areas, the Jura does not run clear with streams and cascades, and on hot summer days the walker will require plenty of liquids. A note is given throughout the route descriptions wherever water supplies may be replenished along the way, and walkers are advised strongly to fill their bottles whenever the opportunity arises. Most of these water supplies will be found at village fountains or cattle troughs fed by a spring. Only those found personally to be of use are noted in the text. Happily, the further south the route takes you, the more frequent the chances are of buying liquid refreshment at farms and chalets that double as restaurants (*Bergwirtschaft*). On these stages the scarcity of water becomes not such a problem, and of course, if you buy a drink at a wayside restaurant you could always ask for a water refill at the same time.

A word about fitness may not be out of place here. It is assumed that anyone setting out to walk the Jura will be a fairly regular recreational walker at home, so they will understand the need to be reasonably fit before undertaking a lengthy walk such as this. Those who have made no effort to get themselves fit prior to tackling the JHR will regret it within an hour of leaving Dielsdorf station, and it will take several days to put right. Every day there are steep ascents and descents to be made, sometimes of well over a thousand metres, and with several hours of travel to sustain over a regularly undulating course, it will be evident that the greater the preparation, the more enjoyable the walk will be. Walking the High Route is an immensely enjoyable experience right from the start, and it can only be devalued if the aches and pains of a lack of fitness are allowed to get in the way. A little preparation at home will help to make the most of the experience once you set out.

As to the best time to tackle the JHR, the summer months of July and August will be the warmest - a point to bear in mind if you tend to suffer from the heat. There are long spells of open ridge-walking and across pastures without any shade. But the wild flowers are splendid and make the walk a colourful experience. Distant views, however, may be disfigured by heat haze for days at a time.

September sees the beginning of frost at night, and when clear spells of weather occur this can be a fine month for walking. But connoisseurs claim October to be best of all, for then the colours of the beechwoods are at their most extravagant, and with frosts dusting the pastures throughout the morning the atmosphere is such that the valleys - and the Mittelland in particular - are lost beneath cloud-seas, and the far-off Alps shine clearly on the horizon.

Towards the closing stages of the High Route, the walker may come across military exercises being undertaken in country traversed by the JHR. (Such exercises are regularly held throughout Switzerland by a conscript army.) In certain instances these may lead to diversions being necessary. Whenever such exercises are due to be held, notices are posted at clearly defined and obvious positions along the route. These are accompanied by a map indicating the affected area. Prior notice of such manoeuvres may be sought from Tourist Information Offices along the way, or on local notice boards in village centres. Telephone enquiries may be made on 024/21 70 59 (Les Rochats area, Stages 10-11) or 021/77 53 51 (Mont Tendre region, Stages 12-14). In both instances these numbers are manned Monday-Friday 7.00-11.45 and 13.00-17.00.

Recommended Maps

Maps of the *Landeskarte der Schweiz* (the Swiss National Survey) are inspiring works of art that cover the country in various scales. Those of most interest to walkers are of either 1:25,000 or 1:50,000 scale. Since the JHR is so well waymarked the 1:50,000 will be quite sufficient - and, of course, considerably fewer sheets will be required than

Jura signpost - no shortage of footpaths!

for those of a larger scale. Those that cover the route of the JHR are listed below:

5005   Seetal-Brugg
5019   Weissenstein-Oberaargau
5016   Bern-Fribourg
241   Val de Travers
242   Avenches
5020   Yverdon les Bains-Lausanne
260   St. Cergue

The specialist Bern publishers, Kümmerly & Frey, have produced a series of special *Wanderkarten* based on the L.S. 1:50,000 sheets with the Jura High Route overprinted in red. These are fine maps that give an easy quick reference to the route. Whilst recommending their use, it must be said that some of the additional information highlighted in red on these sheets (campsites and Youth Hostels, for example) are not always accurate as to either their position or, indeed, even their existence! But the route marking is exemplary. However, they are not so easily obtainable in the U.K. as the standard *Landeskarte der Schweiz* sheets and, when found, are more expensive that the L.S. These maps, under the general title of *Wanderkarte des Jura*, and at a scale of 1:50,000, are listed below:

1 Aargau, Lägeren-Bözberg
2 Basel, Baselland-Olten
3 Solothurn, Delsberg-Pruntrut
4 Neuchâtel, Chasseral-Biel/Bienne
5 Yverdon, Ste. Croix-Val de Travers
6 Lausanne-La Côte, St. Cergue-Vallée de Joux

Addresses of map suppliers in the U.K. and U.S.A. will be found in the Appendix.

Flowers of the Jura

No wanderer along the Jura during early summer could possibly fail to be impressed by the abundance of wild flowers that adorn both woodland path and open meadow. There are several different orchids, campanulas, and the minute blue stars of the snow gentian (*Gentiana nivalis*) tucked in high limestone crags. Martagon lilies, their lovely Turkscap florets wavering in the breeze, will be found in woodland shade and along the edge of high meadows, and the great yellow gentian, tall and stately, is seen almost everywhere between late June and August. In meadows where cattle have not yet grazed, or where the grass has not been mown, polyganums, louseworts and large alpine daisies spill their colours one against another, making these pastures among the brightest corners of the hills, while the exposed limestone shelves cutting through the turf of the crests have their own extravagant species; cushion-spreading androsaces or succulent with fleshy leaves like the sempervivums.

One need not be a trained botanist to appreciate the Jura's flowers. Nor is it necessary to put a name to every plant that is seen. But for those who feel that a little more knowledge would increase their pleasure, Anthony Huxley's *Mountain Flowers* (Blandford Press, 1967) and the Collins paperback, *The Alpine Flowers of Britain and Europe*, by Christopher Grey-Wilson and Marjorie Blamey (Collins, 1979), include most of those likely to be found along the way.

There are one or two Plant Protection Zones along the High Route in which it is an offence to pick any plant found there, and in addition there are several flowers that enjoy complete protection elsewhere in these mountains. (Posters in villages will often be seen illustrating these particular plants.) Clearly not all alpine plants are under threat for their survival, but I would make a plea against picking any wild flower along the way. It is my belief that the best form of collection is through a camera lens. Packet seeds may be bought in certain shops in Switzerland - and from specialist alpine nurseries in the U.K. - by those who would like to plant a reminder of these hills in their gardens at home, and this is likely to prove more successful than an attempt to uproot and transplant, which requires a special licence in any case.

Tread lightly the paths and the pastures with eyes open to the bounty of the hills. The flowers at your feet will then add another dimension to the trek to balance that of the far distant view and the song of the birds.

Practical Information

MEDICAL INSURANCE ought to be taken out by anyone planning to visit Switzerland, since there is no health cover under the EEC form E111 and no state medical health service within the country. Medical treatment is extremely expensive, so insurance cover is strongly advised.

BANKS through which money may be exchanged are normally open from 8.30-16.30, Monday to Friday. In addition exchange facilities are often available at main-line railway stations at weekends.

CURRENCY is in the monetary unit of 100 Centimes (or Rappen in German-speaking regions) = 1 Swiss Franc. Coins are of 5, 10, 20 and 50 Centimes (given as ½ Franc), and 1, 2, and 5 Franc denominations. Notes are of 10, 20, 50, 100, 500, and 1,000 Francs.

POSTAL SERVICES: In the main, Post Offices (PTT) are open during weekdays from 7.30-12.00 and 13.45-18.00. On Saturdays they close at 11.00, with the exception of some main city offices. All Post Offices have *Poste Restante* facilities where correspondence and packages may be addressed for collection by the addressee on production of a means of identity (usually a passport).

PUBLIC TELEPHONES will be found in Post Offices, as well as the standard telephone call boxes that are located in towns and reasonable-sized villages. Automatic STD dialling is the standard feature, so that most places in Europe may be dialled direct. To call a number in Britain from Switzerland dial 00 44 and then the STD code minus the first 0, followed by the individual number required. Instructions in several languages - including English - are usually to be found listed in the booth itself.

IN EMERGENCY dial 117 for Police; 118 in case of Fire. 162 will give you a weather report.

TOURIST INFORMATION OFFICES are to be found in almost every town and tourist resort of any size. In the majority of cases staff speak English and are extremely helpful. They will be pleased to give advice on accommodation, transport etc. and general facilities, but will rarely have detailed information about the condition of paths forming the High Route. Advice should also be sought with regard to the possibility of military exercises being undertaken on sections of the High Route. (See note above.)

SHOP TIMES: Shops are normally open from 8.00-12.00, and from 14.00-18.00, Monday to Friday, but many close on Saturday afternoons at 16.00.

PUBLIC HOLIDAYS: New Year's Day, Good Friday, Easter Monday, Ascension Day, Whit Monday, 1 August (National Day) and 25-26 December. Some cantons also observe one or two other dates.

SUMMERTIME in Switzerland is one hour ahead of British Summer Time, and therefore 2 hours ahead of GMT.

Using the Guide

For the purpose of this guide, the Jura High Route has been divided into fourteen stages of around six hours' walking time each. These stages have been specifically designed to finish either at a place where accommodation may be found, or with reasonable access to it. However, where the route passess a prospective overnight resting place, details are given in order that walkers may break the stage where they see fit, or to coincide with their specific requirements. It should be borne in mind, though, that mention of any hotel, hostel, gasthof, touristenlager, restaurant or café is not intended as an endorsement of the services on offer - which may vary from the most basic to the exclusive.

Distances are given throughout in kilometres and metres, as are heights. These details are taken directly from the map and, with regard to mountain heights, are rounded to the nearest metre where, for example, a summit is given as 1,606.9 (Le Chasseron), it will be quoted as 1,607m.

Times given make no allowance for rest stops or photographic interruptions. Those quoted in the text are accumulations from the starting point of each day's Stage. Inevitably some walkers will find these to be slow, while others may feel they are rather faster than they would choose. My suggestion is that you compare your times with those proposed in this guide and either add to, or subtract from, them for future days. Remember, though, that the JHR is not intended as a pedestrian race track, but as a route to be enjoyed at a leisurely pace.

Route directions are given for the walker heading south-westward, and in route descriptions 'left' and 'right' apply to the direction of travel. However, when used with reference to the banks of streams, 'left' and 'right' indicate the direction of flow, i.e: looking downwards. Where doubts might occur, a compass direction is also given.

Throughout the guide I have sought to give additional information on particularly interesting places and features seen along the way. In the text these are marked with cross-reference numbers which relate to detail given at the conclusion of that Stage's description.

In addition, I have broken the text here and there with brief anecdotal snippets, in an attempt to bring out the flavour of the walk in a manner which no straight route description can. There is nothing dramatic or extraordinary to report, other than the extraordinary nature of the ordinary every-day pleasures to be had by wandering through a delightful countryside. It is my hope that these anecdotes may inspire others to open their eyes and hearts to the glories of the world about them, and that their experience of walking the Jura will be as memorable as mine was for me.

Finally, details contained in this guide apply to conditions experienced during my own walk along the route. Whilst I believe the JHR is likely to remain unchanged in the foreseeable future, alterations do occur from time to time along the trail, for example, when landslips re-shape a hillside - in which eventuality diversions will be adequately waymarked. Amenities may also change from time to time, but hopefully insufficiently to detract from what is a delightful undertaking. Should you find any particularly notable re-routing, or perhaps discover a lodging otherwise not mentioned in this book that you would recommend, I'd very much appreciate a brief note for future editions. A postcard via the publisher would be gratefully received.

* * *

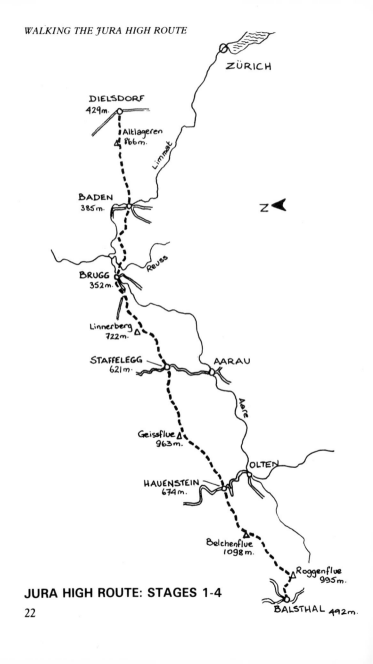

JURA HIGH ROUTE: STAGES 1-4

STAGE 1:
DIELSDORF-BADEN-BRUGG

Distance:	23 kilometres
Time:	6 hours 50 mins.
Start altitude:	429m High point: Altlägeren 866m
Maps:	L.S. 5005 Seetal - Brugg 1:50,000
	K & F 1 Aargau, Lägeren - Bözberg 1:50,000
Accommodation:	Dielsdorf - Hotel
	Baden (4 hrs) - Hotels, Gasthofs, Youth Hostel
	Brugg - Hotels, Gasthofs, Youth Hostel
	And elsewhere along the route. (See text.)

Stage One may conveniently be broken after 4 hours (12.5kms) at the town of Baden, by those still weary from the outward journey from Britain, although the latter part of the stage - other than the initial climb out of the town to Baldegg - is not too arduous or long. There are also several opportunities for refreshment along the way.

As the initial stage of a long walk, it quickly establishes itself with a sharp ascent of wooded hills, gaining almost 440 metres in the first 5 kilometres. It's a peaceful range of hills, with market gardens on the eastern slopes and mixed woodlands on their crowns. Regensberg is one of the loveliest villages of the whole route, and is visited within the first hour. Then there follows a long ridge-walk heading almost due west along the Lägeren with views snatched through the trees, before dropping steeply into Baden, which is crossed through some attractive old streets on the left bank of the River Limmat.

A sharp haul out of Baden brings the route again among woodland shade, and along to a viewpoint on the Gebenstorfer-Horn (514m) overlooking the confluence of the Limmat, Reuss and Aare rivers. Then a quick descent through Gebenstorf for a stroll along the banks of the Reuss, heavy with the meltwater of distant snowpeaks of the Alps, and across to Windisch - marooned between the Reuss and the Aare - for a final riverside walk into historic Brugg.

* * *

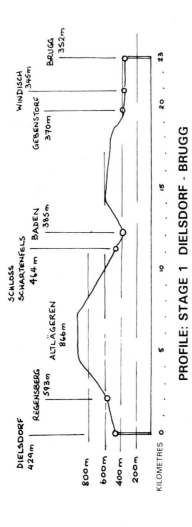

PROFILE: STAGE 1 DIELSDORF - BRUGG

Dielsdorf Station, where the Jura High Route begins.

(1) **DIELSDORF** (429m) *Hotel, restaurant, shops, railway station, Postbuses.*

Opposite the railway station kiosk a signpost indicates the start of the Jura Höhenweg with a finger post directing the way to Regensberg and Baden. Walk up Bahnhofstrasse for about 100 metres, then bear right along Bahnhofweg on a surfaced footpath beside colourful gardens. At a road junction cross over and follow the path behind buildings, leaving the church half-right ahead, and so come to another road where you continue uphill. On reaching a T-junction beside a restaurant, head right and a few metres later cross the road and enter a sloping cobbled street. When this forks, take the right branch - in effect continuing in the same direction - on a footpath beside more attractive gardens and rising quite steeply.

Near the top of the rise you leave the gardens behind, and there is a pleasant view off to the right to other villages nestling in a pastoral landscape; a peaceful view, not dramatic, but gentle and attractive.

Continue ahead through an area of orchards and fields of soft fruit bushes, and at the top of the hill, with a small vineyard to the left and

25

Regensburg, one of the loveliest villages on the JHR.

trees to the right, there is a fine view back to the east, overlooking Dielsdorf and the country beyond. The track continues ahead towards woodlands, winds to the right and forks. The left fork takes the route among trees and bushes and on to the delightful village of Regensberg, a village of immense charm. On reaching the village, turn for a moment to enjoy a broad view.

(2) **REGENSBERG** (593m 40 mins) *Gasthof, restaurants, shops, water supply, Postbuses.*
Walk through the village to the square (an idyllic setting, extremely photogenic) then bear left to pass beneath the archway of Gasthaus zur Krone (date 1541 on one of the pillars) and emerge to a lovely view over a green rolling countryside. There is a panorama board by the road to indicate specific points on view. Continue down this cobbled street among more attractive buildings, and straight ahead at the road junction, now rising uphill. When the road forks branch right for about 200 metres when you will find a footpath heading sharply to the right just after the entrance drive to a house. The waymarked path now climbs among trees and bushes.

The JHR now heads through beechwoods, steadily gaining height and with waymarks wherever an alternative path or track appears.

The track soon goes along a narrowing crest of the ridge with a hint of misted views to the right where the hillside plunges steeply, then a little later the slope falls away to the left. The track brings you to a large water tower and, a few moments later to **HOCHWACHT** (856m 1 hour 40 mins *Refreshments*) a remote building serving as a restaurant.

Continue straight ahead along the ridge, which now becomes more narrow, and pass one or two radio masts. It is a wooded ridge all the way and a flowery stretch too. (Martagon lilies and harebells.) The path leads directly to the viewpoint of **BURGHORN** (859m 2 hours 30 mins).

West of Burghorn waymarks lead the path on, now losing height, still along the ridge and among trees. When you come to an alternative Höhenweg path, take the right-hand one (signposted to Baden in 1 hour 15 mins) which drops through woods in a long descending traverse of the hillside. It eventually follows a broad forest track towards Ennetbaden, waymarked all the way. Along this track you will pass a picnic area on the left, with a water supply, and shortly after a view opens to show the village of Ennetbaden in the valley, with vineyards behind on the hillside.

The broad woodland track swings sharply to the right at a pair of wooden seats and another water supply, but here the JHR goes left on a path that climbs steeply among trees to the restaurant of **SCHLOSS SCHARTENFELS** (464m 3 hours 40 mins *Refreshments*). Pass this and bear right to find the continuing waymarked path now leading down hundreds of concrete steps in the woods. On emerging from the woods, still on steps, there is a magnificent view overlooking the old town of Baden standing by a twist in the Limmat river. A wonderful view of narrow streets, a colourful church spire and the hills beyond. Continue down the steps to street level.

(3) **BADEN**(385m 4 hours) *Hotels, gasthofs, Youth Hostel. All services. Shops, banks etc. Railway station, Postbuses. Tourist information office.*
Use the underpass (signposted to the Bahnhof) to cross the street, and on emerging go over two side streets (sign left to the Jugendherberge -Youth Hostel) and bear right to cross the River Limmat by way of a splendid timber-covered bridge; timber within, and timber without; wooden shingles to the walls and a view to the river beneath the broad planks of the floor. This tunnel of a bridge leads into an interesting street lined with picturesque buildings, and a few metres later bear right along a narrow cobbled street of old stone-walled buildings with

The old town of Baden on the banks of the Limmat.

window boxes bright with geraniums and petunias. A long flight of steps then takes the route up to another underpass and yet more steps at the top of which bear right and follow a footpath (waymarked) past restaurants (on bright days there are people seated outside, and you inch between the tables!) until you come to a pedestrian square with a fountain playing. Turn left into Bahnhofplatz and go through the glass-fronted entrance to an inner shopping area beneath the railway station. Even in here there is a footpath signpost! Follow the walkway to the left of the railway ticket office, and go to Platform 1.

A signpost directs the JHR along Platform 1 (direction of Baldegg and Brugg), and then goes down to another underpass below the railway to emerge at a road which is crossed by way of a zebra crossing, and up a raised footpath ahead. Pass some wooden steps on the right and a few paces later turn right and follow ahead to a very long and wearisome flight of steps. These steps lead out of Baden.

At the top of the steps bear right and walk along a road for about 200 metres. Here the road forks and you take the left-hand branch, passing a large grassy area with a rifle range and tennis courts. The road forks again. Go left once more (water supply at a trough) for a short distance to a footpath slanting left among trees to the edge of woodlands. A track now leads through the woods to a large water tower and, just beyond, the restaurant of **BALDEGG**(568m 4 hours 45 mins; *Refreshments, also accommodation available*).

Walk beside the large restaurant building and turn immediately to the right along a narrow road with woods on either side. Bear right at a junction, and 400 metres later you reach a crossroads where the JHR slants half-left into the woods. The red and yellow diamond-shaped and paint-band waymarks lead ahead, sometimes on broad woodland tracks, sometimes along narrow paths, and bring you to the promontory viewpoint of **GEBENSTORFER-HORN** (514m 5 hours 35 mins). Views from here gaze over treetops to the north to a junction of valleys and rivers, with woods and pastures and towns below.

Leaving Gebenstorfer-Horn bear left and descend through the woods on a narrow path that soon leads past a curious outcrop of conglomerate rocks with one or two caves. Coming to a broad track bear left and follow waymarks to the first houses of Gebenstorf, a fairly modern village. At the end of Hornstrasse a flight of steps lead down to a footbridge over a stream among fine beech trees. Soon you come out of woods and into the village proper, passing a few shops and a church. Opposite a large block of flats a footpath leads to the right, dropping among trees on another flight of steps, over a low road and, by a bus stop, down yet more steps to the right bank of the River

Reuss. Follow the river upstream among trees to a footbridge.

It had been desperately hot up to this point, but the river brought with it a cool rush of air that had the flavour of high mountains in it. A broad, anxious river, full of melting snowfields, it raced northward with an almost frightening power. A flotilla of canoes swept along; then we came to a wall of foam as the river poured over a brace of weirs and we slumped in the grass to enjoy the view. Suddenly a man in swimming trunks ran along the path and onto the bridge...a rubber dinghy had broken loose from its mooring, and as it washed beneath the bridge, so the swimmer leapt from the parapet and with powerful strokes fought the current, caught the dinghy and pulled himself aboard. Then, paddling furiously for the bank, he disappeared from our view. Was it an act of bravery - or utter folly?

Cross the concrete footbridge to the north bank and follow the signs to **WINDISCH** (345m 5 hours 25 mins; *Gasthofs, restaurants*). Go up a cobbled street through the village, over a crossroads and beneath a railway bridge. Turn left along the road beyond this, and after a small housing development leave the road on a footpath heading right beside a beech hedge. It brings you to the banks of the River Aare which you follow upstream.

Ignoring the route off to the left signposted to the Bahnhof, continue alongside the river until the path leads under a modern concrete bridge, and a few metres beyond this waymarks lead up a steep cobbled slope, and along side streets and alleyways to the main street of Brugg.

(4) **BRUGG** (352m 6 hours 50 mins) *Hotels, gasthofs, Youth Hostel. All services. Shops, restaurants, banks, PTT, railway station, Postbuses. Tourist information office.*

*   *   *

Places Visited on the Way:
1. *Dielsdorf:* A medium-sized village of brown-roofed, orange-walled houses set in a quiet and unassuming pastoral landscape; flat and hazy to the east, but wood-covered hills to the west - the start of the Jura.

2. *Regensberg:* One of the most attractive hilltop villages of the whole Jura, it consists of a number of stone-walled houses, some three-storeys high, some with timber framing, some with painted window shutters of an individual pattern. It has a lovely square with a centre piece fountain, and behind it the remaining circular turret of a 13th century castle. Next to it stands the village church. The streets

are cobbled, and from many corners one gains fine views of the surrounding countryside.

3. *Baden:* Once a Habsburg stronghold, Baden is an ancient town with an attractive heart, but a less picturesque industrial sector. As its name suggests, it was once an important spa, enthusiastically described by Thomas Coryate in 1608 who found 'many passing faire yong Ladies and Gentlewomen naked in the bathes with their wooers and favourites in the same'. The sulphur springs were known to the Romans, and even today the thermal pools, both indoor and outdoor, have their devotees. Switzerland's first railway line to be completed entirely within the country, was that between Baden and Zürich which was opened in 1847.

4. *Brugg:* Another Habsburg town with a Roman history, Brugg clusters on the south bank of the Aare. A well-kept place with interesting houses and neat back streets. At the southern end of the town lie the ruins of the Roman military and civil centre known as Vindonissa, which was occupied between AD 9-260. Here was also the forum and an amphitheatre capable of holding 10,000 spectators. In Brugg itself a museum contains a number of Roman relics.

*   *   *

STAGE 2:
BRUGG-LINN-STAFFELEGG

Distance:	15.5 kilometres
Time:	4 hours 10 mins
Start altitude:	352m High point: Linnerberg 722m
Maps:	L.S. 5005 Seetal-Brugg 1:50,000
	K & F 1 Aargau, Lägeren-Bözberg 1:50,000
Accommodation:	Staffelegg - none, but via Postbus (6kms) to:
	Aarau - Hotels, Youth Hostel (in Rombach by
	Aarau)

The shortest day's walking of the whole route, and with a minimum amount of altitude gain, this stage is nonetheless an enjoyable one with plenty of interest. There is only one village actually on the route, but with two more nearby. There are no refreshment facilities available without making a diversion from the JHR, other than canned or bottled drinks bought from a village store early in the day just west of Brugg. Water bottles should be filled before setting out.

Leaving the morning rush of townlife behind, the route soon goes up to the peace of woodlands, then across open farmland on a broad track and over a road to views of the Aare winding away in the south. Forest now leads to a delightful inner land of gentle moulded hills with scoops of valley bright with the chequered patterns of individual meadows and fields. There are cherry trees beside the path and a small village of farms and barns bypassed by our route. More woods with the path climbing to a viewpoint overlooking the Aare Valley, then out to a crest of pastureland, smooth and tended, with forest below and forest ahead, and open coombes with isolated farms scattered among them, and a glimpse of a ruined castle across the meadows.

Another mixture of woodland and pasture brings the High Route to a great bowl of hills: Staffelegg. Unfortunately there is only a restaurant here, and no accommodation to be had. But it is only a short ride south, of about 6kms on the Postbus, to Aarau where a bed can be arranged for the night. (There is a frequent Postbus service along this route, which runs from early morning until late in the evening during the summer.)

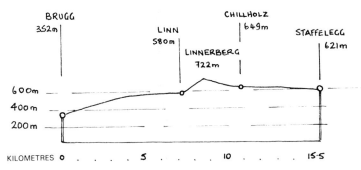

PROFILE: STAGE 2 BRUGG - STAFELEGG

Waymarks and signposts direct the JHR out of Brugg and across the old bridge over the River Aare where you turn left and walk along the road for about 200 metres. Now take a cobbled side road (Renigersteig) slanting uphill. A short distance up this, climb a footpath above the road to the left, up a number of steps among trees. The footpath continues and leads to a crossing path where you bear left on what is a fairly broad track. Follow this round until a few paces before reaching a solitary building, then turn off along a more narrow path which branches half-left ahead, through trees and along what is the edge of the hill slope. It brings you to a broad forest road, at which point bear left along it. Waymarks lead along this for about 250 metres until the *Höhenweg* offers an alternative. One route continues ahead along the forest road to Laufenberg and is, in effect, one of the principal feeder routes of the JHR. *(See below: Feeder Route FR1.)* The other leaves the forest road in favour of a footpath.

Bear half-left here on the footpath signposted to Riniken, Linn and Staffelegg. It takes you among some fine beech trees and eventually comes to a small housing estate which is an outlier of **RINIKEN** (393m *Food store*). Walk ahead along a residential street, at the end of which you come to a staggered crossroads. *(Food store/supermarket on right.)*

Cross the road and walk ahead in the same direction, at first among houses, then a little higher among sloping pastures with views opening before you, and off to the left rolling hills with woodland crowns, and pastures down their slopes with villages tucked in valleys between. On coming to more houses with another minor crossroads, (water supply at a water trough; the last opportunity to fill bottles until 45 mins from

33

Staffelegg) continue ahead on a route signposted to Vier Linden. Waymarks lead through a small housing area and onto a farm track going ahead towards woods and pastures. Wander ahead along the track through open farmland, and soon you will see the village of **VIER LINDEN** (514m 1 hour 15 mins *Gasthof*) across the meadows to the right. A few minutes later you come to another minor crossroads where you turn left and in a few paces reach a busy major road (Basle-Brugg).

Cross the road with due caution, turn right, and immediately beyond a large farm turn left along a farm track which shortly gives some glorious views south along the Aare Valley with wooded hills rolling far off, and orange-roofed villages below.

After 100 metres bear right at a junction of tracks to walk through more open fields with that fine view off to your left. The farm track swings round to bring you back almost to the road again near a farm, then a few paces before coming to the road, branch left on a lesser track heading into forest. Once again you are brought near the road, but on coming to a junction of tracks head left, and left again at the next track junction, then a few paces later bear right at a fork. All the time waymarks are clear.

This forest is a mixed one, with conifers and deciduous species mingling together. The track goes all the way through, and halfway along it you come to crosstracks where once again the JHR has a secondary feeder route coming from the right. *(FR1a. This links with the previous feeder near Oberbözberg.)* Continue ahead on the main track towards Linn, given here as 10 minutes away.

On leaving the forest you cross open farmland and join a narrow country road which leads down left to the little village of **LINN** (580m 1 hour 55 mins *Restaurant*). Without entering Linn the *Höhenweg* branches off half-left at the village sign on a track towards Chillholz. It's a metalled track which slopes up towards woods, then swings right to traverse an open slope of farmland with another lovely view of sweeping countryside to the right, with Linn below; all pastoral and peaceful, as though a living canvas of some 19th century romantic artist brought to life with birds overhead and crickets in the grass at your feet.

The track enters forest again, sweeping in long curves to gain height, but then the JHR leaves the track in favour of a footpath which zig-zags among the trees, climbing to the wooded ridge. The way then cuts below the ridge a little, but rejoins the crest at a little promontory with three bench seats under a canopy of trees overlooking the Aare Valley. This is **LINNERBERG** (722m 2 hours 25mins).

The farming community of Linn, set in a pastoral landscape.

After Linnerberg the path loses height and joins a track descending through the forest to the south-west with the slope falling away to your left. Eventually you leave the forest to cross an open pastureland sloping from a short crest, following still along a clear track.

The sun beat with midday full-summer strength as we crossed the pastures. A farmer was making hay in one of the meadows and the air was filled with the pungent smell of damp grass drying in the sun. Cowbells clattered nearby, but all else was silent. No breeze stirred the leaves. No crickets chirped nor birds sang, nor water to chatter in a streambed. There was a heaviness in the sun that drew all moisture from the earth and instantly evaporated it in the still, energy-sapping heat. There were no clouds, just a shimmering haze that limited distant views. The farmer's wife came along the track carrying his lunch in a wicker basket, and the thought of food made me hungry, so we stretched in the shade of a beech tree and ate bread and cheese while our sweat-soaked shirts dried in the grass. It was good to have an easy day that took from us any sense of urgency about moving on. The day's heat encouraged indolence. We didn't fight it.

In a patch of woodland the track forks, and here you head to the left along a sunken roadway that has cut through the hilltop. Then you emerge with an open view of the few houses and farms of **CHILL-HOLTZ** (649m 3 hours) nestling below in a fine bowl of a valley to the right, and off half-left and some way ahead, the ruined castle of

At the end of Day Two the High Route comes to Staffelegg.

Schenkenberg. At a junction of tracks take the second on the right which will bring you up a green hill enjoying more lovely folding views to both right and left; a peaceful, useful landscape. Overall there hangs an air of calm.

At the head of the hill slope the track swings to the left, then right among forest once more, with several open meadowland patches. At the end of one of these meadow sections a signpost directs the route away from the main track and along a lesser track into forest again. This track broadens and leads for some distance through the trees. Whenever alternatives appear, waymarks direct you along the correct trail. Eventually, as you slope downhill, the track makes a sharp right-hand bend and you will find a water trough on the right. This is the first water supply along the route since just after leaving Riniken. There will be no further supply on this stage, so bottles should be re-filled here.

The forest track leaves the trees at last swinging right near some farm buildings, and you soon join a farm road leading to another, broader, road. Ahead is an interesting and lovely landscape of sharp rising hills and folding hillsides, with knuckle valleys curving away; the whole scene one of manicured splendour. At a road junction with a car park beside it, bear right and follow the road for a few minutes to the pass of Staffelegg.

36

STAFFELEGG (621m 4 hours 10 mins) *Restaurant. Telephone kiosk, Postbuses south to Küttigen (supplies), Rombach (Youth Hostel) and Aarau (hotels, gasthofs, shops, services). (There is a water supply in a lay-by 5 mins walk dwn the road towards Aarau.)*

* * *

Principal Feeder Routes for the JHR:

FR1: Laufenburg-Oberbözberg-Brugg: This, the first of the feeder routes to be met along the main JHR, begins on the Rhine and is of interest to those coming from the Black Forest region of Germany. It is a heavily forested stretch which passes through the tiny village of Sulzerberg (1 hour 25 mins), and thereafter barely touches habitation again until Oberbözberg (3 hours 50 mins). Brugg is reached after 5 hours of walking. (The secondary leg of this feeder (FR1a) parts 1 kilometre north-west of Oberbözberg, and cuts due south to join the main JHR in the forest 10 minutes from Linn.)

* * *

STAGE 3:
STAFFELEGG-GEISSFLUE-HAUENSTEIN

Distance: 20.5 kilometres
Time: 6 hours
Start altitude: 621m   High point: Geissflue 963m
Maps: L.S. 5005 Seetal-Brugg 1:50,000
                   L.S. 5019 Weissenstein-Oberaargau 1:50,000
                   K & F 1 Aargau, Lägeren-Bözberg 1:50,000
                   K & F 2 Basel, Baselland-Olten 1:50,000
Accommodation: Hauenstein - Gasthof, Motel

Much of this stage is spent wandering through forest or woodland, but there are some fine viewpoints overlooking the inner Jura and, given the right conditions, the first real sighting of the Alps. From Wasserflue (844m) and Geissflue (963m) the views are especially memorable. There are open grasslands rich in wild flowers, and towards the end of the day, slopes of pasture sweeping in broad swathes towards the north-west, and gliders sailing overhead.

At Bänkerjoch (674m) and Salhöchi (779m) there are minor road passes to cross, but elsewhere the route wanders over grassy saddles where the only traffic consists of crickets and lizards and grazing cattle. Water supplies are infrequent, but there are one or two opportunities for liquid refreshment at restaurants along the way, and a farm below the Flueberg where you can buy fresh milk straight from the cows!

The Höhenweg follows a series of clear paths and tracks, but there are times when the route leads over broad meadows where the trail is little more than a faint indentation in the grass. Yet even here the way is obvious and should cause no great difficulty.

During the course of this stage the JHR crosses from the canton of Aargau and into that of Solothurn, marked by a stone in the woods.

* * *

At the Staffelegg restaurant bear left and walk down the road (towards Aarau) for about 100 metres, then take the minor road to the

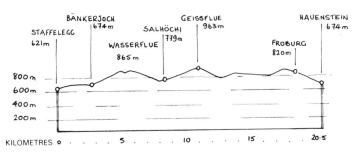

PROFILE: STAGE 3 STAFELEGG - HAUENSTEIN

right, signposted to Herzberg. The road winds through sloping pastures and leads directly to the large collection of buildings of **HERZBERG** (697m 20 mins). *(This is a centre for art and culture, arranging holiday courses etc. Note: Some JHR literature and maps suggest that this is a Jugendherberge - Youth Hostel - but this is incorrect.)*

The road enters a car park, but a lesser track continues ahead towards a large farm. On reaching the farm pass it to your right and continue along the track into lovely beechwoods. Eventually you come out to a minor road at **BÂNKERJOCH** (674m 45 mins *Postbuses*). On the edge of the road there is a water supply; the last for several hours. *(A feeder route for the JHR (FR2) joins here from the little town of Frick. See below.)*

Turn left along the road for 100 metres, then branch away to the right on a track which goes alongside a group of trees, and when it forks head to the left into woods. You soon emerge from these to sloping pastures, and here the track leads round to a saddle in the hills with lovely green views ahead to the west, where hills and valleys fill space with colour, and huddles of buildings slumber in the morning shadow. The track leads on as a belvedere, then at a junction of tracks the JHR heads sharply to the left, almost doubling back on itself, and begins to rise up the hillside. After about 100 metres you desert the track for a path heading up to the right into beechwoods. It climbs in zig-zags and comes to the crest of the ridge where you have a choice to make. The actual continuation of the route follows the ridge to the right, but it is worth leaving rucksacks here for a while to make a diversion to the left along the crest for about 10 minutes to gain the promontory viewpoint of **WASSERFLUE** (844m 1 hour 45 mins). It is a splendid panorama that unfolds before you. Below are the wood-

39

Farm track on the JHR between Bänkerjoch and Wasserflue.

lands and pastures that brought you here, but far off you gaze across untold acres of the Jura, ridge upon ridge, while to the south the hills fall away into the flat expanse of the (1) **MITTELLAND** whose horizon is blocked by the snowy Alps.

To continue the JHR, follow the crest path heading west, narrow in places, but always wooded, to its western promontory. It then zig-zags down to a broad forest track which in turn leads to the upper edge of pastures with the farms of Salhöchi seen ahead. You will come to a pass road near a restaurant at **SALHÖCHI** (779m 2 hours 35 mins *Refreshments*), and immediately beyond this, take a track to the left heading into forest.

For about 50 minutes you follow the track, then a path, through the forest. Beside the path there are wild strawberries and raspberries and, later in the year, blackberries to eat - the free harvest of the hills. The path leads up to the ridge, passing on the way the marker indicating the border between cantons. This ridge is not as narrow as that of the Wasserflue, but it is still interesting, with snatches of views through trees, but at **GEISSFLUE** (963m 3 hours 25 mins) there is a glorious vista of spreading Jura hills far away to the north-west. *Here, on a perch of the crest, you look down to the villages of Oltingen, Wenslingen and Anwil, and out to chequered fields striped here and there from the cutting of hay, or from a variety of cereal crops; out to grassy hills and ridges, out to forests and individual stands of trees; and off to the north*

40

where, so they say, on a clear day you can see the Black Forest. Even when the far views are limited by heat haze, it is still a magnificent panorama. And among the limestone rocks at your feet there grow sprays of wild flowers. A lovely spot for a picnic lunch.

The path from Geissflue takes you down through the forest in tight zig-zags, and out by the Naturfreundehaus at **SCHAFMATT** (840m 3 hours 40 mins), an opening of pasture looking out to the south. *(Here another feeder route of the JHR (FR3) links with the main trail, having come from Rheinfelden. See details below.) (Note: When the Naturfreundehaus is open - infrequently - it may be possible to arrange accommodation for the night. Details unknown.)*

Pass in front of the Naturfreundehaus along a track, and 100 metres later bear right down a series of steps through a pastureland and onto a narrow metalled road where you turn right. *(Note: for refreshments, bear left here for 5 minutes to reach a restaurant.)* Continue along the road to an open saddle of meadows where you come to a T junction and bear left for 100 metres. There follows a fork. Take the right branch and soon go left on a track which leads into forest shade.

On emerging from the forest you cross another open grassy saddle with a new valley system opening to your right, and with a number of hay barns strung in a line on the hillside ahead. This is all very lovely country. The path leading from here is initially a true belevedere giving fine views into a fold of hillside leading to a village in a neat criss-cross pattern of fields and meadows, and with another village far off moulding into a welter of haze.

The trail goes along the edge of forest, and at a junction of tracks the waymarked High Route goes straight ahead on a narrow path between the tracks and up among trees. You soon come out of the trees to cross a high open pastureland devoid of shade.

Other than at Schafmatt, where we'd suffered in the crossing of the meadowland saddle, we'd managed to cope with the heat as there had been so much forest shade. But now, in early afternoon, the sun was at maximum roast and we staggered across these high pastures longing for water, for shade, for a cloud to drift our way and give a moment's respite. Nothing came, and we followed a long hedgerow - curiously English in the heart of Swiss Jura - towards a mirage of shadow that formed a scant blob of darkness from a solitary tree. Off to our left we could look through a funnel of hills to the Mittelland and the industrial area outside Olten, while the rough meadow went on and on, shadeless, sun-bleached, and our water bottles merely contained the last drops of moisture we were loathe to drain. But at the far end of the meadow the slope dropped to a farm road, and there gurgled the most wonderful sound of the day - water from a cattle

41

trough. Ankle-deep in cattle-churned mud we drank our fill, topped the bottles and headed away again refreshed, seeing the country around us now with new eyes and a fresh appreciation.

Cross the long pastureland heading south-west, and drop down at the far end to a farm road. (Water supplies.) Here we turn right and follow the road towards a solitary farm. (More water supplies from a pipe feeding animal troughs, and the possibility of buying fresh milk.) The route makes a diversion round the farm, then heads up grassy slopes behind it, following a line of telegraph poles to a saddle. Here yet another new landscape opens out. Lovely conical-shaped hills, some with pastures, some with woods, with little indented valleys squeezed between them. A track now leads round through woodland shade, then out near a large transmitter station. Continue ahead towards the buildings of **FROBERG** (820m 5 hours 25 mins *Hotel*).

Leave the track shortly before Froberg, and go to the right along the right-hand edge of a sloping meadow. This then brings you to a road which swings round and goes all the way to Hauenstein; but after about 700 metres a Höhenweg path heads off to the left into woods as an alternative to the road. It winds through these woodlands, drops down to a forest track and then takes you to the right to reach the road once more. Here turn left and a few paces later you come into the village of Hauenstein.

HAUENSTEIN   (674m 6 hours)   *Gasthof, Motel, restaurants. Post-buses (to Olten). Water supply.*

*   *   *

Things Seen on the Way
1. *The Mittelland:*   One of the dominant features seen from many of the ridges of the Jura, the Mittelland is a broad plain, largely agricultural, that stretches from the eastern limits of the Jura to the foothills of the high Alps. The contrast of this great flat expanse of farmland against the rolling, pastoral hills, adds a considerable amount to the scenic pleasures of the JHR.

*   *   *

Feeder Routes for the JHR:
FR2: Frick-Junkholz-Bänkerjoch: The first of the feeder routes to join the main route on Stage 3, this is a short link of only 2 hours 45 mins, which leads for about 10.5 kilometres from the little town of

Frick - the last Habsburg possession in Switzerland. The route leads south into a narrow wooded valley, steadily gaining height to Stock-matt (710m) shortly before joining the main JHR at Bänkerjoch.

FR3: Rheinfelden-Farnsburg-Schafmatt: This is really a two-stage link totalling some 34 kilometres. Rheinfelden sits on the south bank of the Rhine looking across to Germany. An ancient town with its picturesque corners, it has hotel accommodation and good Postbus and rail connections. The JHR link route heads south through woods and open farmland to Hersberg (2 hours 15 mins) where it then veers eastward on an undulating course to Farnsburg (5 hours 20 mins). Shortly after this the path swings to the south once more, into woods again to the village of Anwil (588m 8 hours 5 mins), then rising for a further 6kms. to join the main route at Schafmatt by the Natur-freundehaus.

*   *   *

Martagon lilies - Gifts of the Jura

STAGE 4:
HAUENSTEIN-BARENWIL-BALSTHAL

Distance: 20.5 kilometres
Time: 6 hours 30 mins
Start altitude: 674m   High point: Belchenflue 1,098m
Maps: L.S. 5019 Weissenstein-Oberaargau 1:50,000
                   K & F 2 Basel, Baselland-Olten 1:50,000
Accommodation: Balsthal - Hotels

A lovely day's walking; scenic, colourful, ever-varied and interesting, in which the high point is reached with some ease along a generously-graded track, although steeper ascents have to be made later.

The walk begins among woods, but when you emerge there are some splendid soft-country views with white cliffs of exposed limestone rising from forest and meadow. A track, engineered by Swiss soldiers during the First World War, leads steadily up towards the Belchenflue, and when this is traded for footpath, another delightful hillside of pasture and farm takes the Höhenweg to a forest section that finally gives way to a broad and quiet valley, with the village of Bärenwil occupying a privileged position among the meadows.

South-west of Bärenwil the route climbs steeply in woods again, but suddenly the path comes out of the trees, crosses an enclosed meadow, swings through a gap and comes onto the glorious green rolling ridge of hills that is the very essence of the Jura. Wandering along this broad crest, one gazes north across successive ranges of grass-clad hills, and south to the deep flatlands of the so-called Mittelland, to the long line of the Alps.

The ridge leads on for about 6 kilometres, at first open and pastoral, then wooded with a steep ascent of the Roggenschnarz (up an interminable flight of timber-strengthened steps), then reaches the dramatic viewpoint of the Roggenflue (995m) before descending to the town of Balsthal.

Water supplies are not such a problem during this stage, and there are opportunities for other refreshment at restaurants or cafés along the way. But walkers are advised in any case to begin the day with a full water bottle.

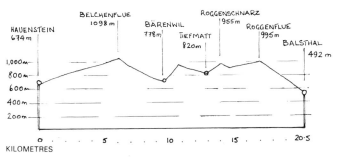

PROFILE: STAGE 4 HAUENSTEIN - BALSTHAL

A few metres south of the road by which you entered Hauenstein, a minor road heads off to the west, signposted to Ifenthal. (Water supply here.) Walk along this road, but shortly after bear right on a waymarked track that takes you past a number of farms. About 500 metres along this track branch left along another which leads into forest of the Ifleter Berg. When you come out of the forest you emerge onto the pastoral saddle of **CHALLHÖCHI** (847m 1 hour) with lovely views ahead. Follow a metalled road, which soon becomes a track winding into woodlands, then out to open pastures with the wooded hills standing ahead in interesting formations.

The view from Challhöchi.

Path leading south from Belchenflue.

The track takes you into more woods and soon begins to climb. It is efficient and well-engineered, the product of various battalions of Swiss soldiers during the First World War, and along the route a number of regimental insignia have been carved into the rock walls and painted brightly. These insignia add another interest to the day's journey. Steadily height is gained by way of this unsurfaced road, and eventually, where it makes a sharp right-hand bend at **BELCHEN-FLUE** (1,098m 2 hours), you will see a small turnstile on the left taking the JHR onto a footpath.

(At this point another JHR feeder route (FR4) joins the main route, having started in Liestal. This same feeder is linked about 400 metres north-west of Belchenflue with an Alternative JHR (A1) which runs on a more northern traverse of the Jura via Delémont and is, in turn, joined by a direct route from Basle. See details below.)

Wander down this narrow footpath enjoying the views ahead through a funnel of valley to the village of Langenbruck tucked below. Down a series of steps the path brings you to a grassy saddle where it forks. Bear right and continue downhill beside a line of trees and wild roses towards a farm. Shortly before reaching the farm (*refreshments available*) fork left and go uphill towards woodlands, and you will soon come to a pastureland with several converging paths - not all of which are clear on the ground. Turn sharply to the right at a signpost and descend through the centre of the pasture to enter forest at a waymarked fence. A clear path now leads down through the forest and onto a track. Bear left and follow this track for about 500 metres, keeping a lookout for a waymark that will direct the route onto a narrow path dropping steeply through the trees on the right. It takes you into a valley bed where you bear left alongside a stream and go through a narrow limestone defile. Suddenly the path comes out to a surprise of open pastureland and the farm of **ASP** (772m 2 hours 40 mins), a most attractive place; a secluded sweep of meadow enclosed by forest.

Continue beyond Asp, now on a track which soon forks. (A good opportunity to fill water bottles at the cascading stream here.) Take the right branch of the track, in effect continuing ahead in the same direction. This curves round, passes a farm or two, then comes to the open smiling pastures of the Cholersbach Valley, at the head of which nestles the neat little village of Bärenwil.

(1) **BÄRENWIL** (778m 3 hours) *Restaurant, Postbuses (to Langenbruck and Hägendorf), water supply.*

Cross through Bärenwil and take the minor road south, passing a

Bärenwil, - a small hamlet on Stage Four of the High Route.

water trough on your left. Very soon up this road a track branches to the right, signposted to Tiefmatt, Roggenflue and Balsthal. Follow along this until, shortly after, waymarks direct you off the track and onto a path climbing left through the woods. This path is narrow at first, but it broadens and, at one point, actually climbs what amounts to a rather novel ladder of wooden steps. Continue steeply through the woods and then emerge to a high enclosed patch of meadow. Wander across this to find a waymarked track opposite which heads half-left among trees and comes out a moment later to a huge panorama. Here you look south over the Mittelland with its strips of agriculture colouring a fertile plain, and way off to the snow-capped Alps; and off to the right to a lovely gentle landscape of hills and valleys of the Jura, with an undulating green pastureland ridge dividing the two.

The air was full. Full of sound - of birds and crickets and cowbells. Full of fragrance as the meadow ahead had just been cut and was now drying in the sun. We wandered through it, our boots scuffing at the hay and sending mini-clouds of seeds sparkling around us; insects flying away or leaping for cover. Then beyond the first meadows a hedge swept down to the right, and growing alongside it were martagon lilies with butterflies drifting first from one, then another, and lizards sunning themselves nearby. Below us stood the remains of the castle of Alt Bechburg, and beyond that, in the valley cut by the Augstbach river, the village of Holderbank where, according to the map, there should be a campsite. (That evening, after a long and frustrating diversion, we discovered the map's betrayal.) We wandered on, thoroughly enjoying the contrasting views to north and south, and lured by the hills ahead. This, it seemed to me, was the Jura at its best, and I was well content. (Later, of course, we were to discover many other faces of the range, each of which had its own particular claim to being the real Jura; each of which had its own devotees and enthusiastic supporters, and I was forced to admit that the Jura's charms were even more varied that I'd imagined.)

Bear right in the saddle of pasture and follow along the grassy ridge with contrasting views to the left and right. This ridge takes you for some way across meadows and along lines of trees, first on the right, then on the left. You come onto a track and then to a short stretch of country road which leads to the **BERGWIRTSCHAFT TIEFMATT** (820m 4 hours 5 mins *Refreshments*).

Continue beyond this along the road that becomes a track through a patch of forest. Out of the forest you are faced with a steep open pasture with a path climbing up to yet more forest. *(On the way up this, pause for a moment to enjoy the glorious views behind, overlooking the grassy ridge over which you have been wandering.)* The steep path works its way through the forest and goes up hundreds of timber-reinforced steps on the ascent of the **ROGGENSCHNARZ** (955m), from the top of which there is another fine viewpoint. Having gained the ridge you soon descend a little to a wooded saddle (908m), then amble ahead regaining height gently through what is a very pleasant forest. It is difficult to believe, as you wander along this path, that you are at almost 1,000 metres, but as the ridge narrows, so hinted views shine through the trees as a reminder of the great drop to the south. Eventually you pass a couple of bench seats and come to the end of the ridge at a prominent viewpoint on a limestone cliff. This is **ROGGEN-FLUE** (995m 5 hours 15 mins). From it you overlook the flatlands to the south with Oensingen directly below, and off to the peaks of the Alps. A wonderful panorama.

Now take the continuing path steeply down through the trees, then sweeping in long broad curves across pastures to forest once again. In places the waymarks are a little faint, but once in the forest the way is clear. The path leads to a track, and the track comes out to the town of Balsthal, with the waymarks leading left along streets to reach the station.

(2) **BALSTHAL** (492m 6 hours 30 mins) *Hotels. All services. Shops, restaurants, banks, PTT, railway station, Postbuses.*

* * *

Places Visited on the Way

1. *Bärenwil:* A small village set in a gentle saddle of meadowland on a minor pass linking the valleys of the Vorderer Frenke and Augstbach with the lowlands to the south. Postbuses serve the village and go to Hägendorf and Langenbruck. Pleasant wooded hills rise to north and south of the village, and if it only had overnight facilities, Bärenwil would make a very pleasant walking centre.

2. *Balsthal:* Built on the site of a Roman settlement (the Parish Church occupies ground where a Roman villa once stood), the town centre is a mixture of old and new. On the outskirts to the north-east, the road to Mümliswil squeezes through a limestone 'gateway' below the remains of the 12th century castle of Neu-Falkenstein. To the south rises the steep wooded ridge of Wannenflue.

* * *

Feeder Routes for the JHR:

FR4: Liestal-Ramlinsburg-Belchenflue: Liestal is an industrial town on a junction of valleys a little to the south-east of Basle, with which it has rail links. From it two feeder routes set out; the first runs south for almost 20 kilometres, steadily gaining height (it has more than 750 metres to ascend) before it joins the main JHR after 5 hours 25 mins at Belchenflue.

FR5a: Liestal-Lupsingen-Passwang: This feeder takes the walker from Liestal through rising country west of FR4 to join the Alternative JHR northern loop (A1) on the ridge of Passwang (1,204m), or, by joining FR5b (below) continues as far as Belchenflue for the main JHR. This stage crosses the Baselbieter Jura over some 20.5 kilometres, in about 5 hours 50 mins.

FR5b: Passwang-Langenbruck-Belchenflue: A suitable link by which feeder routes FR5a and FR6 may join the main route, this follows a sharply undulating course for almost 13 kilometres, taking some 4 hours 25 mins. Accommodation in Langenbruck (3 hours).

FR6: Dornach (Basle)-Seewen-Passwang: For those coming direct from Basle it is possible, by combining this route with FR5b, to join the main High Route at Belchenflue. (For the Alternative JHR starting at Dornach, see A2 below.) Dornach to Passwang is a long (7 hours 25 mins) stage of 25 kilometres, rising from 294m to 1,204m. It links with FR5a at Holzenberg, and the two routes are then identical for the last 11 kilometres.

Alternative JHR Routes are outlined elsewhere in this guide, after the main Stage descriptions of the High Route.

*   *   *

*Regimental crest on track
to Belchenflue*

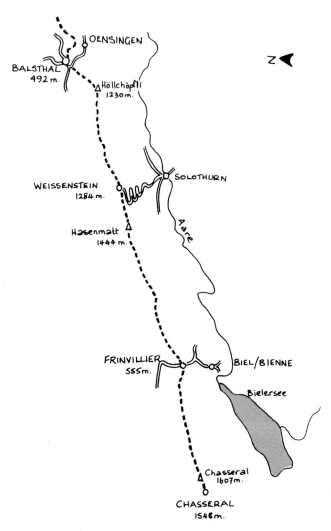

JURA HIGH ROUTE: STAGES 5-7

STAGE 5:
BALSTHAL-BÄTTLERCHÜCHI-WEISSENSTEIN

Distance:	20.5 kilometres
Time:	6 hours 15 mins
Start altitude:	492m High point: Weissenstein 1,284m
Maps:	L.S. 5019 Weissenstein-Oberaargau 1:50,000
	K & F 2 Basel, Baselland-Olten 1:50,000
	K & F 3 Solothurn, Delsberg-Pruntrut 1:50,000
Accommodation:	Weissenstein - Hotel, Touristenlager (dormitories)
	And elsewhere along the route. (See text)

A day of ridge walking, through forest and across open pastures with fine views.

It begins with a steep ascent of the Höllchöpfli (a rise of over 700 metres), mostly in woodland, but opening with broad vistas here and there. The crest of the ridge is followed along the Schattenberg, keeping above the thousand-metre contour all day. When the ridge is deserted in favour of meadows, the route wanders below a limestone wall, then works up among trees to a high grassy saddle. It's all lovely country; lush, flower-strewn, cared-for. More woodlands, more pastures. Then the route comes to Ober Balmberg, a popular spot with local folk from Solothurn who can get here by Postbus for a day's walking or a picnic. An hour's walking from the road brings you to the large hotel at Weissenstein overlooking the great plains to the south - and the magical views of the Alps.

Weissenstein is ski-country. There are signs of the downhill enthusiast's requirement for uphill machinery. There's a chair-lift, too, going down to Oberdorf near Solothurn, and a road that winds in countless zig-zags into the valley. Rarely will the walker arrive at this point and find solitude, for it's accessible and well-known to locals who flock here at weekends and during the holiday season. After a day's remote hill walking, Weissenstein comes as a link with civilisation. But there's refreshment and a bed for the night. And a panorama to woo the senses.

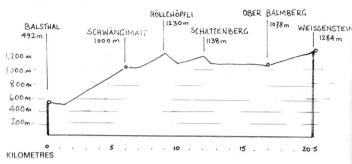

PROFILE: STAGE 5 BALSTHAL - WEISSENSTEIN

From the station in Balsthal head south-west beside the railway line, and shortly after cross over to the left, then bear right to walk along a side street parallel with the rails. At the end of the street you come to a main road opposite Thalbrücke station. Turn left and follow the road for about 100 metres, then cross to the right and enter Lebernweg, a street that crosses the railway and soon after passes a factory. When the road forks take the left branch alongside forest. You soon leave the road and enter the forest on a track that climbs in long sweeps, gaining height easily. But after a while a waymarked path heads directly up the slope, still in forest, and speeds the heartbeat somewhat. Later, at about the 800 metre contour, the steep path rejoins the forest track where you bear right, soon to cut away left on another path. This leads to a surfaced road which you leave at the first hairpin bend to make a short cut, and when the road is rejoined, it is then followed all the way to Schwängimatt, a large farm with pleasant views overlooking the Jura hills to the north. (This is a very popular hang gliding and para-gliding centre, and you may be fortunate in seeing enthusiasts flying from here.)

SCHWÄNGIMATT (1,000m 2 hours *Restaurant, dormitory accommodation.*)
A path leads past Schwängimatt and crosses the pastureland heading south-westwards towards rising forest. You will soon gain extensive views south over the Mittelland, then follow the path into forest and up to the narrow crest of the ridge along a screen of trees.

The ridge path leads eventually to a military fence, and just beyond this you come to the viewpoint of **HÖLLCHÖPFLI** (1,230m 2 hours 45 mins) which overlooks the south.

54

Morning mist - Schwangimatt.

The waymarked path descends steeply on a flight of stone steps on the southern side of the ridge, still among trees. It then works along through the forest and out to a broad pasture. (Halfway across this, below the path to the left, there is a source of fresh water at a pipe serving a cattle trough.) Cross the pasture and come to a junction of tracks where the *Höhenweg* offers a choice of routes. This is **HINTEREGG** (1,079m 3 hours 10 mins).

The narrow road going straight ahead allows a low-level diversion, pastoral in quality and with the possibility of refreshment (at the Bergwirt-schaft nearby, and at Vorderer Schmidenmatt in 40 mins), and rejoins the higher route a short distance from Hofbergli, about 1 hour 40 mins from this junction. It is waymarked throughout and easy to follow. (Note. Touristen-lager accommodation is available at both Hinteregg and Vorderer Schmid-enmatt.)

Our route takes the higher path along the crest of the ridge. Bear half-left and traverse a rough pasture slope towards trees where a proper path then leads along, or just below, the crest of the ridge. Every now and then a cleft in the limestone of the ridge reveals surprise views of pastures far below, and distant mountains hovering in the sky. Towards the end of this Schattenberg ridge you have a splendid view down to the right into valley pastures where the lower route travels, and through a limestone defile (Horngraben) to the

55

village of Matzendorf. You will soon come then to the crestpoint of **SCHATTENBERG** (1,138m 4 hours), and shortly after the path swings off the ridge and descends to the left, passing beside a huge slab of limestone, still in the woods, and comes to crosspaths. Continue straight ahead, dropping a few metres onto a narrow country road with a huge view over the lowlands to the south. Bear right for a few paces to pass through a cleft in the limestone ridge. This is **BÄTTLERCHÜCHI** (1,074m 4 hours 15 mins). Immediately through this head to the left on a path among trees.

Once again the path follows just below the crest of the ridge; an undulating crest with sudden views. It brings you to a track and continues ahead over green pastures that now straddle the ridge. Soon you are walking below a line of white limestone cliffs with little trees on them. Cliffs that form another continuing section of ridge to the north. There are lovely rolling hills ahead, and to the left once more a great plunge into the lowlands.

There were hawks wheeling overhead now, their shadows flashing in black arrows across the pastures, the sun dazzling on the limestone and a breeze to temper the excesses of the afternoon. For hour after hour we had been treated to the luxury of a world we had all to ourselves, but we were willing to share it with others now that we could see Hofbergli ahead, knowing that this hill farm would be adding to its income by doubling as a restaurant. 'A Sinalco stop' when the sun shone was always a good excuse to remove the rucksack and enjoy just sitting with a cold drink. Enjoying the peace, a moment to allow the heart to settle its pace, reminding us that this, after all, was a holiday.

The track leads directly to **HOFBERGLI** (1,065m 4 hours 50 mins *Refreshments*). Almost immediately after the farm the track forks. Take the right-hand trail which swings round through more pastures and then gains height among trees, before emerging later at a high grassy saddle. The path then crosses these pastures and heads down towards a new landscape, entering more woodland, then out again to an open rolling green crest with a farm and the large Kurhaus Balmberg seen below. Beyond rises a steep forest-clad hill (Röti, 1,396m) from which the Weissenstein projects westward, but unseen from this point.

On reaching the farm bear right on a track leading through trees to a narrow metalled road. This is Ober Balmberg, and for refreshments and accommodation you bear left for 5 minutes to the Kurhaus.

OBER BALMBERG (1,078m 5 hours 15 mins *Refreshments. Hotel accommodation*).

To continue to the Weissenstein, cross the road and follow a clear track ahead going though pastures. On the far side the track enters forest and continues to wind its way at a steady angle, eventually bringing you out to a wide pasture saddle across which can be seen the Weissenstein Kurhaus, with a T.V. transmitter mast behind it. The track comes to a junction of paths. Continue ahead on the main track which will take you to the Kurhaus.

(1) **WEISSENSTEIN** (1,284m 6 hours 15 mins) *Accommodation in bedrooms and dormitories. Restaurant service. Chair-lift (and road) down to village of Oberdorf (train and Postbus to Solothurn) for shops, banks, all services.*

* * *

Places Visited on the Way
1. *Weissenstein:* Well-known and extremely popular with local Swiss from the plains, it is a popular excursion for families, school-parties and individual walkers. The restaurant is very busy - both inside and out on the terrace in good weather, where the views are extensive. It was from the heights of the Weissenstein that Hilaire Belloc (in *The Path to Rome*) captured his first view of the Alps; a view whose description is among the most often quoted pieces of travelling literature:

> 'For there below me, thousands of feet below me, was what seemed an illimitable plain; at the end of that world was an horizon, and the dim bluish sky that overhangs an horizon... One saw the sky beyond the edge of the world getting purer as the vault rose. But right up - a belt in that empyrean - ran peak and field and needle of intense ice, remote from the world. Sky beneath them and sky above them a steadfast legion...'

STAGE 6:
WEISSENSTEIN-GRENCHENBERG-
FRINVILLIER

Distance:	24 kilometres
Time:	6 hours 30 mins
Start altitude:	1,284m High point: Hasenmatt 1,444m
Maps:	L.S. 5019 Weissenstein-Oberaargau 1:50,000
	L.S. 5016 Bern-Fribourg 1:50,000
	K & F 3 Solothurn, Delsberg-Pruntrut 1:50,000
	K & F 4 Neuchâtel, Chasseral-Bienne 1:50,000
Accommodation:	Frinvillier - Hotel
	And elsewhere along the route. (See text)

During this Stage the High Route passes from the canton of Solothurn to that of Berne, from German-speaking Switzerland to that part of the country which is dominated by the French language. Although the country-side remains very similar to that of the more easterly Jura ranges, the architecture of farms and villages begins to show an influence more akin to that of France than the more traditionally Swiss with which we have grown familiar. There will, of course, be variations, but on the whole the route now adopts something of a French character as the borders of the two countries steadily draw closer to the JHR. And during the coming days signposts will change from bearing the German inscription, Höhenweg, to Chemin des Crêtes. Waymarks, of course, remain as before.

The early part of the walk goes through forest and leads onto the crest of the ridge, but then this ridge becomes something of an escarpment, falling steeply to the south, sloping gently in broad grasslands to the north in shallow pastoral valleys. This escarpment, in turn, gives way once more to a brief crest which unfolds to open meadows lavish with wild flowers. There are farms here, and Bergwirtschaften giving the opportunity for refreshment before tackling the next region of pasture that will present another enormous panorama overlooking the south.

Another stretch of forest and pasture, with more farms and distant views. Then an extensive, almost parkland, region (Pres de la Montagne) through

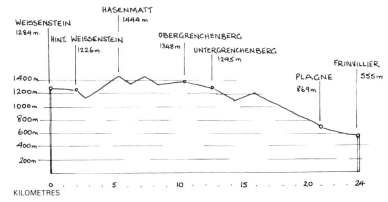

PROFILE: STAGE 6 WEISSENSTEIN - FRINVILLIER

which a clear track leads eventually to the village of Plagne, a pleasant collection of houses and with the opportunity for overnight accommodation. From here another hour's walking, almost all of it downhill, takes the JHR into the deep bowl of hillside, laced with road-bridges and tunnels, in which squats Frinvillier.

*   *   *

From the Kurhaus Hotel Weissenstein wander up the road to a junction of tracks, and follow that which is signposted to Hinterer Weissenstein. A few paces later turn off the main track and take the waymarked footpath along the edge of trees, and in about half an hour you will come to the Restaurant/Gasthof Hinterer Weissenstein.

HINTERER WEISSENSTEIN (1,226m 30 mins *Restaurant, accommodation in bedrooms and dormitories*)
Pass in front of the restaurant along a broad track for a few metres actually heading south-east. On coming to a junction of tracks bear right. (Water supply here.) The track soon forks and you continue straight ahead along the right branch which leads towards woods. A few paces after having gone through a gateway, bear half-left on a waymarked footpath among trees. This soon becomes a rough forest track, then turning off it you climb a long flight of log-reinforced steps to gain height quickly. At the top of the steps the path levels off to follow the wooded crest of the ridge, then descends to an unsurfaced

59

roadway at a minor pass (1,315m). Cross this road and continue up the other side on a further stretch of waymarked path signposted to Hasenmatt in 25 minutes.

Climbing steeply among the trees the path regains the ridge, then out to a sloping pasture (a very flowery area) just to the left of the crest, then down a little to a junction of paths. This is **HASENMATT** (1,444m 1 hour 40 mins). (The ridge a little above it represents the highest point of the Solothurn Jura.) Turn right here and descend a little way on the northern side of the ridge to another path junction.

Head left to cross a grassy slope, then on coming to a track turn left and a few metres later, when it forks, bear right. In a few paces bear left again on a waymarked path heading up a slope of rough pasture and following a line of telegraph poles. The trail winds among trees, then comes onto a broad rolling green ridge where splendid views are to be had (so they say). This is **STALLFLUE** (1,414m 2 hours 15 mins).

Clouds were all around us. They boiled up from the valleys to deny us the views we felt certain would be enormous. All we had was a damp grey curtain drawn closed for the morning. There was a drystone wall built of rough limestone blocks to follow across an unseen landscape and to save our dropping over the edge, and as we set off along its line the wind suddenly blew in cold gusts to give a momentary view of the minor Jura ridges and high valleys to the north. It was a frustrating view, for there was much to absorb and to enjoy. But it was not to be, for the curtain of vapour was pulled to once more, and we continued on our blinkered way in ignorance.

This almost-escarpment region has a steep drop to the south, while the northern slopes are more gentle. The limestone wall to follow goes to the south-west, then when it begins to lose height you veer half-right, then towards a fence on your left, beyond which the ridge plunges suddenly. There are fine views into a bowl of pastureland with a couple of buildings in it way below, and out to the Mittelland with the River Aare seen winding snake-like through it. *(A window had appeared through the curtain of mist to enable us to capture this intimate vista.)*

The ridge leads on and becomes rather narrow, the waymarked path maintaining interest all the way along it. It comes down to a slender saddle, then climbs with the upward ridge on an undulating course, gradually leaving the crest and coming to a large open pastureland with the buildings of Oberer Grenchenberg occupying a prominent position in it. The footpath leads over the grassland and comes to a narrow road a short distance from the buildings.

OBERER GRENCHENBERG (1,348m 3 hours *Restaurant, dormitory accommodation*)
Unless you require refreshments or accommodation, bear left on the little metalled roadway and a few minutes later desert this in favour of a footpath heading to the left up a sloping pasture. Ahead you will soon see a lofty radio mast. The path leads to a track, still heading through pastures in which there are a few items of ski machinery. Follow the track down to another restaurant building (water supply at a trough).

UNTERER GRENCHENBERG (1,295m 3 hours 25 mins *Restaurant, accommodation in bedrooms and dormitories*)
Passing the restaurant to your right wander down the road which serves it, with a very splendid panorama spread before you gazing out to the south to the Alps. The road winds down and enters forest. A few metres later bear right on a waymarked footpath which makes a short cut and rejoins the road soon after. In a few more metres leave the road once more on the continuing path heading left through the forest, emerging to yet another stunning view over the south. Cross the pasture slope to the restaurant/farm of **STIERENBERG** (1,075m 3 hours 45 mins *Refreshments*) which you pass on your left, and walk up the roadway beyond it until you come to a car park. (Just before reaching the car park there is a water supply on your right.)

Head left along a track, and when it forks soon after, take the left-hand branch into forest. Before long you bear right on a climbing path which brings you past a pair of marker stones indicating the border between the cantons of Solothurn and Bern. A little beyond this the path comes to the edge of the forest and heads across a series of rough pastures, now merely a vague grassy trail. It leads to another farm that serves also as a restaurant, **MONTAGNE de ROMONT** (1,120m 4 hours 40 mins *Refreshments*).

Continue beyond this to take a track veering right through a gateway at a signpost directing to Plagne and Frinvillier. This leads for some distance through an almost English-style parkland. Eventually the track comes to a number of isolated holiday chalets half-hidden to either side, then after a while another direction post sends you off to the left along a footpath leading down through woodlands. The path becomes a track, leaves the woods and heads across an open farmland to reach the little village of Plagne.

61

PLAGNE (869m 5 hours 35 mins)   *Hotel, Auberge, Restaurant. PTT. Postbuses. Water supply.*

Turn right at the crossroads beside the Post Office and wander up the road; then, on reaching a hotel, the road forks. Take the left-hand branch which soon becomes a track. A waymarked path then leaves this to cross pastures on the left, following a somewhat devious course and entering a forest, now on a clear trail. Follow this down to a road where the path runs on a parallel route a little above it before crossing to the south side and descending to a second road. Bear right along this, and on reaching a junction of roads go half-right on a footpath descending among trees. This leads down to Frinvillier. Follow waymarks down into the village. The only hotel here is set beside the road as you walk through.

FRINVILLIER (555m 6 hours 30 mins)   *Hotel, restaurant. PTT. Water supply. Rail and Postbus links with Biel/Bienne (Hotels, Youth Hostel. All services, shops, banks.)*

*   *   *

STAGE 7:
FRINVILLIER-LES COLISSES-CHASSERAL

Distance: 18.5 kilometres
Time: 6 hours
Start altitude: 555m   High point: Chasseral summit 1,607m
Maps: L.S. 5016 Bern-Fribourg 1:50,000
                     K & F 4 Neuchâtel, Chasseral-Bienne 1:50,000
Accommodation: Chasseral - Hotel

On this section of the route a long and steady climb is made to the summit of Chasseral - the highest point of the Bernese Jura - from which a great spread of countryside is laid out. It begins with a very sharp ascent out of Frinvillier's deep bowl; a steep haul on a forest path straight after breakfast, gaining almost 600 metres before the slope relents. There follows a series of tracks through high meadows and past farms, over pasturelands with big views and flowers at your feet.

There is a CAS (Club Alpin Suisse) hut in a lovely position, (the Jurahaus) but it is not always open, so it cannot be relied upon for accommodation. (Members of the CAS arrange to pick up the key from Biel/Bienne.)

From the Jurahaus more pastures, more grassy slopes and yet more farms are passed on the way up to Chasseral. Tracks and paths, sometimes a little sporadic with waymarks, take the High Route onto the ridge just before the summit where a huge transmitter tower dominates the surrounding countryside. Descending a little to the south-west the route comes to a large restaurant and hotel where a night's lodging can be had with a wonderful view over the Lac de Neuchâtel far below, and off to Mont Blanc and the high Alps. A popular place with visitors to Neuchâtel, it is in some ways reminiscent of the Weissenstein at the end of Stage 5.

Note: There is an Alternative Stage from Frinvillier to Chasseral, taking a more gradual route which is outlined below, after the main JHR Stage description.

* * *

The route out of Frinvillier heads west along the road towards a

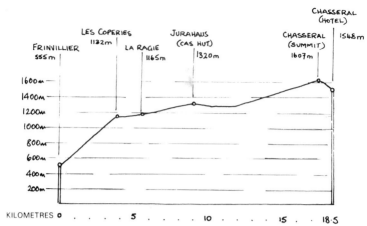

PROFILE: STAGE 7 FRINVILLIER - CHASSERAL

modern road bridge. Immediately after crossing a river (La Suze) turn right on a waymarked path that climbs steeply into the forest. It is a zig-zag path, narrow in places, but always clear and with an occasional glimpse of the tight valley of La Suze below to the north.

After about fifty minutes or so you approach a broad forest road, but without joining it turn right onto a continuation of the waymarked path. This follows up the crest of the ridge with views again down into the valley, but then the ridge broadens, you emerge from the trees and head up a steep strip of meadowland, at the top of which join a track and bear right. At first across open pasture, then among trees, then over more pastures, the track leads up to a little farm, **LES COPERIES** (1,132m 1 hour 45 mins).

Continue ahead along the track which winds among rough meadows and comes to another isolated high farm, **LA RAGIE** (1,165m), where you bear half-left on the continuing track. At the first bend after La Ragie the track forks and you take the right branch. A short distance along this you will come to a large water trough fed by a spring of clear water. *This is the last guaranteed opportunity to refill water bottles during this stage.*

On coming to a grassy saddle bear half-left across it to join another track, and a few paces later go through a small gate, then half-right across a pastureland. The path is very faint here on the ground, but marker posts point in the right direction and take you to a track

64

heading through some trees and out to another narrow pasture. A very faint path now heads up the right-hand side of this pasture, and over a rise into a much larger grassland area (an extremely fine flower meadow), where off to your left you will see another farm, **PRE CARREL** (1,295m).

Waymarks lead away to the right, then left to head through more pastureland, now on the north side of the ridge, gaining height a little before swinging back to the left. Although the path is not always evident on the ground, there are plenty of waymarks to lead you to the CAS hut.

CABANE JURAHAUS (1,320m 3 hours 10 mins *Open infrequently. Temporary voluntary guardian. 70 dormitory places. Meals when guardian in residence. Drinks for sale. Water supply*).

It had been raining when we left Frinvillier, and it was raining still when we arrived at the hut. The fragrance of woodsmoke reached us before we could see it, and we went inside optimistic of warmth and hopeful of drying out. We did; steam-dried by the stove, discussing with the guardian the route ahead, poring over the map, searching for other huts along the way for the future. There was no-one else at this hut, and when we looked through the register, we could find no other British names at all. Had none from the U.K. been here in the past two years? Or more? The guardian peered disconsolately at the rain sweeping across the meadows beyond the window, and reckoned he was in for a quiet weekend. We would willingly have changed all that, had the hut been higher on the mountain, or we'd arrived later in the afternoon. But as it was, it was still too early to contemplate something of value to be wrung from even the most foul of days. If you look long enough for beauty, you'll find it. Anyone can feel dejected at times such as these, but if you know how to enjoy the wild days, you'll be rewarded. I was well content.

Continue beyond the hut on a trail among open pastures, and soon after, bear right on a path across more pastures to reach a clear track. This track swings to the right and you leave it to walk ahead, soon passing a small timber-built cross-country ski chalet on your right. A short distance beyond this you will come to a junction of unmade roads at **CRÊTE du CHASSERAL** (1,288m 3 hours 40 mins). Cross straight ahead and take a vague grassy trail (signposted) up a sloping pasture. This brings you to a clear track that goes up among trees, then leads to a farm, **LES COLISSES du HAUT** (1,325m 4 hours 10 mins).

The track leads on, gaining height over grass and among trees, and

On the JHR near Chasseral.

becomes in places a narrow trail. Although the waymarking over this section is sometimes a little sporadic, the route is obvious enough. It eventually works onto the crest of the ridge (falling steeply to the right, sloping less dramatically to the left) and goes up to the high point of **CHASSERAL** (1,607m 5 hours 45 mins), which is topped by an enormous transmitter tower. A panorama board here details the major features of the view.

Wander ahead, passing directly beneath the tower, and follow the road beyond. After a short stretch on the road the path heads up the slope ahead and over the brow of hill on the ridge before coming onto the road again and reaching the hotel.

HOTEL CHASSERAL (1,548m 6 hours)   *Hotel, restaurant. Kiosk-type foods on sale - chocolate etc. Chair-lift (to Nods, and Postbus from there to Lamboing and Lignières - Hotels). Postbuses (north to St. Immier; infrequent).*

Alternative Stage:
JHR7a: Frinvillier-Les Prés-d'Orvin-Chasseral: This option takes a less-demanding route from Frinvillier, heading first to the edge of the village of Orvin (716m 1 hour 10 mins. Hotel accommodation), before rising steadily through the pastures of Les Pres-d'Orvin, and joining the main JHR at the minor crossroads of Crête du Chasseral (1,288m 3 hours). From here to the Hotel Chasseral the routing is the same as that for Stage 7. Total time for this Alternative Stage: 5 hours 20 mins.

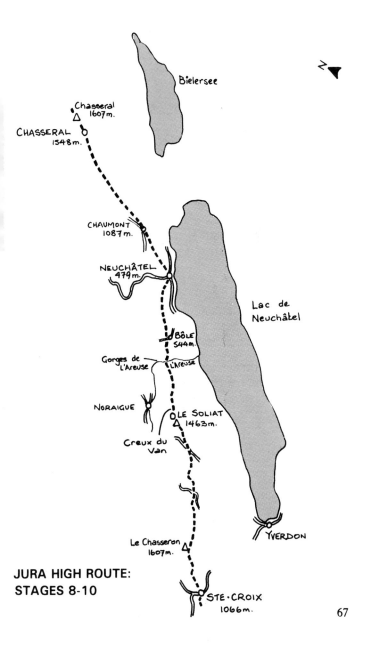

N

Bielersee

Chasseral
△ 1607 m.

CHASSERAL
1548 m.

CHAUMONT
1087 m.

NEUCHÂTEL
479 m.

BÔLE
544 m.

Gorges de
L'Areuse

L'Areuse

Lac de
Neuchâtel

NORAIGUE

LE SOLIAT
△ 1463 m.

Creux du
Van

Le Chasseron
1607 m. △

YVERDON

**JURA HIGH ROUTE:
STAGES 8-10**

STE·CROIX
1066 m.

67

STAGE 8:
CHASSERAL-CHAUMONT-NEUCHÂTEL

Distance:	21 kilometres
Time:	5 hours
Start altitude:	1,548m Low point: Neuchâtel 479m
Maps:	L.S. 5016 Bern-Fribourg 1:50,000
	K & F 4 Neuchâtel, Chasseral-Bienne 1:50,000
Accommodation:	Neuchâtel - Hotels, Youth Hostel
	And elsewhere along the route. (See text)

After the long ascent to Chasseral from Frinvillier, this Stage is almost all downhill to the lakeside town of Neuchâtel. Given good weather there are pleasant views to enjoy as you wander south-westwards to the great plain with its foreground of lake and backcloth of the Alps. There's a lot of altitude to lose, but it is mostly on a gentle gradient with only a few short sections with sufficient angle to give the knees a twinge.

Initially the day begins with a ridge walk overlooking a splendid panorama, but then the way descends through a lush vegetation and over meadows and past numerous little farms. Now and again there are patches of woodland, but mostly the route is in the open as it crosses grasslands rich in wild flowers again. There's a short stretch of country road walking (a little over a kilometre of it) near Les Trois Cheminees, and some attractive isolated houses to pass. Then you come out of woodland near Chaumont to a surprise view of the broad expanse of the Lac de Neuchâtel below, before dropping through forest on the final approach to the town.

For those in need of hotel accommodation, it will be necessary to descend all the way into town, but those planning to stay at the Youth Hostel can avoid entering Neuchâtel proper by continuing along the JHR which skirts its upper reaches. This takes you within about 50 metres of the hostel.

Note: Chasseral offers an approach to the Alternative Route which swings on a more northerly course towards Vue des Alpes, and in addition is linked by a Feeder Route (FR7) from La Ferrière. (Outline details are given below, after the main JHR Stage descriptions.)

Note: There are no opportunities en route for topping-up water bottles, but several prospective refreshment stops at farms doubling as restaurants. (See text.)

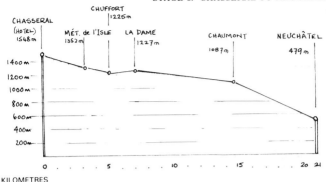

KILOMETRES

PROFILE: STAGE 8 CHASSERAL - NEUCHÂTEL

Leave Hotel Chasseral and head west along the road for a few paces before striking off on a waymarked path leading onto the ridge at the entrance to a plant protection area. Wander along the limestone crest which plunges steeply on the right (north) and gives lovely views in both directions.

After a day of rain and low cloud we were anxious to study the sky first thing in the morning, and were rewarded with a cloud sea spread beneath us and huge banks of cumulus rolling far off. There was a promise of better things to come, and as we left the hotel and began to walk along the crest in the cool wind of morning, so that promise was being fulfilled. Now we could see views that had been denied us yesterday, and there was a whole new world to enjoy. Steeply to the north the ridge plunged to pastures where cattle grazed, and we looked through a cleft in a secondary ridge to the village of Villeret deep in the Vallon de St.-Imier, and far beyond that to sparkling hills of green that folded out of Switzerland and into France. Strips of low mist hid some of their valleys from us, while out to the south there were only hints of the glories yet to come as more clouds swept along beneath our perch. But it was clear to us that the weather was attempting to mend its ways, and we were confident that it would do so. We therefore faced the day with renewed optimism.

The crest path leads down to a minor road junction that forms a pass at 1,502 metres. (The road heads north to St.-Imier, and south to Nods and Neuchâtel.) Cross the road and regain the crest of the ridge once more. But the path soon loses height among a lush and somewhat tangled vegetation, then joins a farm track which leads to the little hill farm of **MÉTERRIE de l'ISLE** (1,352m 45 mins. *Refreshments*).

We were caught on the path of an international 32 kilometre fell race

69

Jura hay barn on the walk from Chasseral to Neuchâtel.

(Chaumont-Chasseral-Chaumont), and throughout the morning we would repeatedly need to side-step rather hurriedly from the route as competitors -in various degrees of exhaustion - staggered past. This first farm was a feeding station, and a cheering crowd had gathered there to encourage the runners and to hand out drinks. They accepted our presence as an amusing addition to their day - but offered us no refreshment!

Continue beyond the farm along the track which winds down a slope, then take a waymarked trail heading half-right shortly after reaching the foot of the slope. This brings you in about 35 minutes to another farm, Chuffort.

CHUFFORT (1,225m 1 hour 10 mins. *Refreshments. Touristen-lager.)*
Beyond Chuffort you cross more pastureland towards some woods, and on passing through these the track swings to yet another farm, **LA DAME** (1,227m 1 hour 40 mins *Refreshments*) where the route passes under an arch made by a barn attached to the farm building. Now the track veers to the right and reaches a narrow country road. Turn right here and follow this road for a short distance, passing another farm on the left and then entering woodland. A few paces later bear left on a waymarked path climbing steeply for a moment among the trees. It soon levels and, before long, comes to a large clearing of pasture with a

number of farm buildings in it. Just before coming to the first of these, bear half-right across a hillock of pasture, keeping a slope of trees to your right. There is no real path to be seen on the ground, but a few waymarks will direct you. Soon you come to a vague path ahead among trees, and this leads down through tree-scattered pastures and comes to a stone-built barn. Passing along the right-hand side of this, veer half-left beyond it and, after about 100 metres, enter more woodland on a clear trail. This soon becomes a broad woodland track, and on emerging from the trees go straight ahead across a brief meadowland to a narrow road with one or two farm buildings scattered about.

Cross the road to the left of a little house, and follow a faint path half-left across pastureland among isolated trees. The grassy trail brings you beside an attractive farm, into trees once more, then out to another country road where you turn right. Passing several pleasant houses continue along the road, taking the left branch where it forks, and soon reach a minor crossroads at **LES TROIS CHÉMINEES** (1,133m). Walk ahead still for a further 500 metres through an avenue of lime trees and past some more farms, then turn left on a waymarked track which soon goes into a forest.

About 100 metres inside this, bear right on another waymarked path that comes to a large field almost entirely surrounded by forest. Cross the field, bear left and walk beside it before entering the forest again. A clear track leads through and eventually brings you out to a pasture by some houses. Cross a narrow road and continue ahead in the same direction to a neat farm, **MÉTERRIE d'HAUTERIVE** (1,180m) where you turn left and follow an obvious track through another section of forest, which then leads out to the edge of Chaumont beside a chapel. Turn left on the road, and in a few paces there is a splendid view left down to the Lac de Neuchâtel and the Alps far beyond. Walk along the road into Chaumont.

(1) **CHAUMONT** (1,087m 3 hours 20 mins.) *Hotels, restaurant, small shop. Funicular railway to Neuchâtel.*
With a large grassy area on your right bear left on a waymarked side road, and onto a track heading into woods. It is waymarked all the way to Neuchâtel, and takes you through a large woodland area, past a farm and along a track to a road. Bear left along the road for about 50 metres, then left again on a path through more woods. Eventually you are brought to a road again where you turn right and follow to crossroads at Les Cadolles on the edge of Neuchâtel.

For hotel acommodation and all services, turn left and walk

downhill along the road (signposted for traffic to Bern and Biel). For Youth Hostel accommodation see Stage 9.

(2) **NEUCHÂTEL** (479m 5 hours) *Hotels, gasthofs, Youth Hostel. All services. PTT, shops, banks etc. Railway station, Postbuses. Tourist Information Office.*

* * *

Places Visited on the Way

1. *Chaumont:* A pleasant, rather scattered village in a sunny position on the hillside about 6 kilometres from Neuchâtel, it is growing with a number of new developments. Fine views overlooking the south; funicular access with Neuchâtel.

2. *Neuchâtel:* An old town (built on Celtic foundations) and capital of the French-speaking canton, it is attractively fashioned on steep slopes above an extensive lake which, somehow, gives it a Riviera atmosphere. There are vineyards along the northern shores of the lake on the outskirts of town, but in the bustling heart of the place there are all the services and amenities associated with a busy centre of commerce and tourism. Among the tourist attractions there are museums of art and archaeology, a 13th century castle and Collegiate church.

* * *

STAGE 9:
NEUCHÂTEL-BÔLE-LE SOLIAT

Distance:	23.5 kilometres
Time:	6 hours 30 mins
Start altitude:	479m High point: Le Soliat 1,463m
Maps	L.S. 242 Avenches 1:50,000
	L.S. 5020 Yverdon-les-Bains-Lausanne 1:50,000
	K & F 5 Yverdon, St.-Croix-Val de Travers
	1:50,000
Accommodation:	Le Soliat -Touristenlager
	And elsewhere along the route. (See text)

The high isolation of Le Soliat comes as a welcome relief after the frenetic bustle of town. Up there one can enjoy huge vistas and feel the joy of open spaces. Up there the great limestone amphitheatre of the Creux du Van forms an impressive centre-piece, while to one side stretches a length of limestone pavement in a semi-moorland. Space is the essential feature of this high plateau, whether you visit in summer or winter, and from it the walker can gaze back over the previous two days' journey in one single glance, and ahead to new horizons that beckon. The route to Le Soliat, however, involves a lengthy mixture of suburb and forest, with a brief introduction to the cool confines of the Gorges de l'Areuse - the lower reaches of the Creux du Van's great shaft.

From Neuchâtel the route hugs the borderline between suburb and forest above the villages of Peseux and Corcelles. (Those who chose to stay overnight at the Youth Hostel can buy provisions and use banking facilities by little more than a short diversion from the JHR at Peseux.) Then beside a small area of vineyards, and through open farmland and woods on the way to Bôle. Just beyond here open farmland gives more views over the Lac de Neuchâtel. Then it's into woods and suddenly a breath of cool air comes sweeping from the right as you enter the Gorges de l'Areuse; a region of green. Green trees, green moss-covered rocks, green water. Even the air seems to be tinged with green. An almost sub-aquatic atmosphere.

Steeply the route now climbs into forest on path and track for a little under a thousand metres. The first opportunity for refreshment does not come

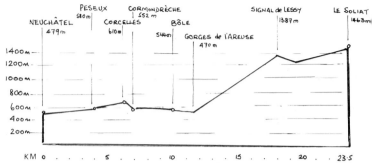

PROFILE: STAGE 9 NEUCHÂTEL - LE SOLIAT

until you've been in forest for nearly three hours, but when it does there's a sense of relief, for above the little farm/restaurant trees give way to open pasture as you enter the Creux du Van Nature Reserve, and big views open out. There then follows a pleasant stretch of meadowland and patchy wood as the final uphill approach is made to the summit of Le Soliat along the rim of the cirque. It is one of the magical places of the Jura High Route, and is well worth savouring.

Note: Fresh water supplies are scarce on this Stage.

* * *

Those who stayed overnight in Neuchâtel can either retrace their steps back to the crossroads near Les Cadolles, or take a bus (route No.9).

At the crossroads at Les Cadolles head west (continuing in the same direction as when you entered from Chaumont) and walk along this road above the town. There are occasional waymarks on lampposts etc., and the JHR finger posts giving directions. At the next major road junction (a little more than a kilometre from Les Cadolles), bear right along a road heading to Pontarlier, and shortly after this branch half-right on a minor road signposted to Le Chanet. There are JHR waymarks. After 100 metres go up a flight of steps which brings you to the Rue de Suchiez. *(The Auberge de la Jeunesse - Youth Hostel - stands about 50 metres along this to the right.)* Cross the street and continue up more steps. They lead to a steeply climbing street which in turn brings you to a track heading into woods. (Signposts directing to Cormon-drèche, Bôle and Le Soliat.)

Skirting the lower edge of the woods the track forks and you bear right. When you come to crosstracks by the entrance to an enclosed reservoir, cross straight over onto a minor track, still among trees. On reaching a road bear left and soon come out of the woods to a view of the lake across the rooftops of Peseux. Continue ahead at a junction of roads (for Peseux, drop downhill left for 5 mins) and when the road forks take the right branch along the edge of woodlands.

PESEUX (565m 40 mins) *Hotel. Shops, banks, PTT. Postbus, railway.*

Beside woods and houses the road leads to another junction where you bear right. At the next fork veer half-left along a path beside woodlands, and this brings you to yet another road where you go left. On reaching another junction bear left, and 50 metres later go right and immediately after passing a garage, head left along a narrow lane dropping downhill. This brings you to a railway line (water supply shortly before it), and 100 metres later you turn right along a residential street. This leads to a cemetery which you skirt, climbing uphill soon among houses again. Waymarks continue ahead past these, then off through vineyards and open fields with woods before you and views left to the Lac de Neuchâtel and the Alps beyond.

The road leads through woods, across more farmland, and on coming to yet more woods a waymarked path directs you to the right on a curving journey among the trees, then out across an open field to the edge of the railway at Bôle.

BÔLE (544m 2 hours) *Hotel, railway, Postbus.*

Bear right along a track beside the railway, and at a minor road head left across the lines, then immediately across these go to the right along a side street. This takes you past some pleasant houses with good views over vineyards and farmland sweeping away towards the lake, which is now becoming more distant. On coming to a T-junction bear left and a few paces later head to the right on a waymarked path into woods. In a few minutes you will come to the (1) **GORGES de l'AREUSE** (470m).

There is a wooden footbridge across the narrows of the gorge where the river has come rushing through the defile over countless thousands of years, smoothing the rocks into curves and hollows, swirling beneath a canopy of trees. A most attractive setting. Cool and green, with fish clamouring beneath the bridge.

Cross the bridge and climb the stepped path beyond. It takes you into forest, crosses an open glade and enters forest once more. Waymarked throughout, the route is sometimes along a narrow path,

On Stage Nine, the JHR crosses the River l'Areuse in a narrow gorge before climbing steeply to Le Soliat.

sometimes forest track, sometimes even a surfaced road. Much height has to be gained, and on occasion there are surprise views to be had out to the lake seen through a screen of trees.

Eventually you emerge from the forest by the car park of the Creux du Van Nature Reserve and take the road going uphill. In a few paces you come to a little farm/restaurant on the left, a neat single storey building in a tranquil setting, with the Lac de Neuchâtel seen through the trees.

LA FRUITIÈRE de BEVAIX (1,235m 4 hours 50 mins) *Refreshments, Touristenlager.*
The route continues beyond the farm and heads up pastures into trees once more. There follows a lovely stretch of pastureland broken here and there with spinneys of trees; the trail winding up to the edge of what seems to be a green escarpment with the northern slope dropping into the valley which contains the Gorges de l'Areuse. The path brings you to **SIGNAL de LESSY** (1,387m), marked by a large wooden cross, with the great drop to the valley below where Rousseau stayed

76

The limestone cirque of the Creux du Van.

for inspiration in September 1764. There's a view to the Creux du Van, and rolling green hills folding into the distance. A delightful spot.

We sat for a few minutes enjoying the views and the peace. But that peace was shattered by low-flying swifts that came hurtling across the depths of the valley shrieking, as they do. There were dozens of them; high-speed arrows in black and white. Presumably they had their nests in the limestone wall below and were perturbed by our presence, for they swooped at us, wheeled away and returned to bomb us again. Time and again they attacked us in squadrons out of the sun. Taking the hint we shouldered the rucksacks and continued on our way - cowards, or sensitive to the concern of the birds?

The waymarked trail continues through more pastureland, then descends to an open meadow of flowers, passes a hut on the right and joins a forest track that leads to a narrow road in a forest-enclosed pasture with another distant view of the Alps. This road comes eventually to the farm/restaurant of La Grand Vy.

LA GRAND VY (1,381m 6 hours)   *Refreshments, touristenlager (20 places) and accommodation in bedrooms (10 beds).*
The path goes beyond the farm, winds through more rough pastures and a few trees, and comes to the very edge of the white limestone cirque of the (2) **CREUX du VAN**. As you wander along the lip of the amphitheatre it is difficult to appreciate the full enormity of it, and it takes some minutes before you can come to terms with its size. To the left the upper pastures have a certain moorland quality about them, and there are stretches of limestone pavement exposed through the flower-speckled turf. Across these pastures stands a signpost marking the summit of **LE SOLIAT** (1,463m 6 hours 30 mins). A gap in the drystone wall at the head of the cirque gives access to it.

Note: For touristenlager accommodation at the nearby farm, **FERME du SOLIAT** (1,382m 6 hours 50 mins. *Refreshments, tourist-enlager*), continue round the rim of the cirque for about 10 minutes beyond the gap in the drystone wall that gives access to Le Soliat's summit, then find another gap in the wall. Go through and walk across the open pasture to the isolated farm seen away to the left. (About twenty minutes from the head of the cirque.)

It rained that evening, but when we'd eaten the rain stopped and we went out to have another look at the cirque. Clouds were being spirited around and below us as we strolled along the rim once more; mist bubbling as though in a witch's cauldron, webs of fantasy becoming torn and tattered on the cliffs under our feet. And then a brocken spectre was cast into that mist and for the first time in my life I wore a halo; my own personal multi-hued

Creux du Van and the high plateau of La Bied.

halo; a completely circular rainbow, with my own shadow imprisoned by it. Turning away from the cirque we went over to Le Soliat and saw far in the distance the glimmer of Lac Léman and felt that we were nearing the end of the journey. But what really took my attention was the light; that sparkling evening light, crisp yet soft, it shone on isolated pastures way in the distance, picking out isolated farms and twists of unknown rivers and stands of trees on a far-off hill. The great high plateau of Le Bied had rolls of cumulus fluffed over it, but sweeping up to it from the west came banks of dark, threatening cloud, momentarily blotting out the descending sun that valiantly edged those clouds with gold. Tomorrow's hills were dark in shadow. There was the smell of rain in the air. But we had that hour of magic with the Creux du Van and its mist, with the light and the distant views, and went back to a mattress in the attic of a dark barn thankful for another good day.

*   *   *

Things Seen Along the Way
1. *Gorges de l'Areuse:* The upper reaches of the Val de Travers are broad, flat-bottomed pastures through which the River l'Areuse curls its way. But at Noraigue the valley walls form a pincer-like squeezing (the Creux du Van rises to the south), and the lower portion of the valley becomes a deep cut through the green-clothed limestone. East of Champ du Moulin the gorges begin in earnest, with the river broiling and gouging its route through. There are paths on both north and south banks of the gorges, from which to explore the fine cascades and an attractive bridge at Pont Dessus.
2. *Creux du Van:* A remarkable limestone amphitheatre, some 500 metres deep, cutting into the Jura crest east of Le Soliat. It is 1,200 metres wide and 2 kilometres long, and its walls form a most attractive sight from above and below. A steep path, starting from Ferme Robert, climbs the south-eastern wall and joins the main JHR path a little west of La Grand Vy. The depths of the cirque are densely forested, but the head of it is soft moorland-like pasture with limestone pavement showing through. A Nature Reserve (designated in 1972), there are ibex, chamois and marmots here, and typical limestone-loving plants. Rock climbing on the walls of the cirque is restricted to specified periods.

*   *   *

STAGE 10:
LE SOLIAT-LE CHASSERON-SAINTE-CROIX

Distance: 24 kilometres

Time: 6 hours 30 mins

Start altitude: 1,463m   High point: Le Chasseron 1,607m

Maps: L.S. 241 Val de Travers 1:50,000

               L.S. 5020 Yverdon-les-Bains-Lausanne 1:50,000
               K & F 5 Yverdon, Ste-Croix-Val de Travers
                 1:50,000

Accommodation: Sainte-Croix - Hotels, Youth Hostel
                And elsewhere along the route. (See text)

This section of the route passes through a military training area. On occasion exercises are carried out here which effectively close the path for half a day or so. Notices are posted at strategic points warning of path closures at specified times, and in such instances it will be necessary to work out an alternative portion of the route. (Sketch maps on posts indicate the particular region where the exercises will take place, so with the aid of your map you should be able to plan an alternative.) Advance notice may be gained from enquiry at certain Tourist Information Offices along the way. Enquiries by post should be addressed to: Office de Co-ordination 1, Case postale 498, CH 1400 Yverdon; or telephone 024/21 70 59.

This is an undulating Stage, losing height gradually at first, then steadily rising to a high point on the ridge at Le Chasseron, which comes as a welcome surprise after five hours of walking. The descent from here is gentle to begin with, then fairly steep into the tidy village of Sainte-Croix.

It is a day of pasture and woodland, of quiet roads and back-country farmland. A day with no water supplies en route, but with several opportunities for liquid refreshment at farms and cafés.

*   *   *

From the finger post on the moorland summit of Le Soliat, walk in

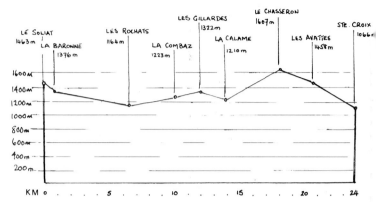

PROFILE: STAGE 10 LE SOLIAT - STE. CROIX

a south-westerly direction along a faint sign of footpath in the grass, and down a large open pasture to reach a crossing track near a farm building. (The track coming from the right leads from Ferme du Soliat.) Bear left along it through more pastures to come upon a clear farm track where you turn right towards **LA BARONNE** (1,376m) *Refreshments*). Turn left immediately before the farm, go down a slope and bear right through pastures, following a trail towards some trees. (10 mins from La Baronne on hilltop left is the CAS hut-Cabanne Perrenoud, open weekends.)

A clear track now brings you through more pastures and trees. Waymarks are given wherever a junction of tracks offer alternatives, and after more than a kilometre you will reach a narrow surfaced road where you turn left. Following this road for about one kilometre you then bear half-left along a stony track that runs parallel with the road, but a little later returns you onto the road once more. Some 200 metres later turn right into a lay-by and through a gateway into a large pastureland. (In this lay-by there is a notice board beneath a signpost giving details of any restrictions imposed by military exercises.)

Waymarks lead along a vague grassy trail in an arc over the pastures, and then enter a woodland, now on a clear path. On emerging from the woods cross an enclosed pasture and enter forest on the far side. The path leads ahead and eventually comes onto a country road where you bear right.

It was raining again. Clouds squatted on the trees like broody hens and everywhere was washed in grey. As we came through the forest near the road we passed a group of conscript soldiers huddling together waiting for a signal to begin their exercise. They looked totally miserable as they crouched in the wet grass, capes pulled tightly over their shoulders, the rain dripping through the trees onto them. Prospects for the day were not good for these poor souls, and I had a great deal of sympathy for their plight. We shared the same weather, the same wet pastures and forests, the same dank forecast; yet there was one major difference - choice. We were out in the cool, windswept rain because we chose to be. It was therefore acceptable to us and we were happy enough, while the young soldiers had no option but to do as they were directed, rain or no. Without pausing in our stride we simply acknowledged their presence, left them to their misery and wandered on.

Along the road you pass some army buildings, then come to a large restaurant on the right; Café les Rochats.

LES ROCHATS (1,164m 1 hour 35 mins) *Refreshments, touristen-lager accommodation.*
Continue along the road until it makes a sharp hairpin bend to the right, then leave it in favour of a broad forest track going ahead for about one kilometre. It is a clear track all the way through the forest, but when it brings you to the edge of the trees, so leaving the military area, go out to a meadow with a large building standing at the head of the slope. Cross the meadow to a point about 40 metres to the left of the building, go through a wall and up to a stony track where you bear left. Follow along this track through open pastureland for a little over a kilometre until you reach a road. Turn left and walk along this for about 500 metres, as far as a restaurant set beside the road in a green sweep of meadowland. This is **LA COMBAZ** (1,223m 2 hours 30 mins. *Refreshments.*)

It was tempting to stop here for coffee, so we took our rucksacks off outside and shook the excesses of the morning's weather from our water-proofs. Suddenly the restaurant door opened and out rushed the lady proprietor. With a great deal of hand-flapping and an out-pouring of mis-placed sympathy, she opened the garage and hung our cagoules and over-trousers over a drying frame, then scuttled us into the warm coffee-fragrant restaurant with a non-stop monologue of sorrow. Before we could take a seat she practically tore the soaking shirts from our backs, strung them over her cooker to dry and insisted we then wore her husband's jacket and pullover; neither of which fitted. But we sat happily in the warmth beside a steamed-up window, sleeves halfway up our arms, eating home-made pastries and drinking strong hot coffee as the clouds squeezed the last of their contents onto the meadows outside. I thought of the soldiers crawling through the forest in their war game, and reckoned we'd struck it lucky.

Bear right alongside the restaurant and go up a slope of pasture following waymarks into a patch of forest. A path leads through, crosses a minor road and continues in forest again until you come to a long open meadow. Walk the length of this towards **LES GILLARDES** (1,322m) a farm which you pass about 40 metres away on your right. A narrow road now leads left down through more pastures, a little like a parkland area. The road swings to the left and a track heads away to the right. Follow the track whose waymarks lead into yet more pasturelands. Just before coming to another farm, **LA CALAME** (1,210m), bear half-right and follow along a grassy trail with waymarks for about ten minutes, then you will reach a neat farm building overlooking the south; **LA CRUCHAUDE** (1,223m 3 hours 40 mins).

Bear right and wander up the slope, through trees and up a second slope towards yet another farm, **LES CERNETS-DESSOUS** (1,357m). At the top of this slope of pasture pause for a moment to enjoy the fine view back over much rolling country. Bear left along a line of waymarks that takes you to a grassy trail leading to a road junction. Cross over and continue ahead along a narrow country road for about 500 metres. Then, when it curves sharply to the right, leave it to go up a grassy trough on the left, at the top of which you suddenly have a splendid wide view south and with the summit of Le Chasseron about 600 metres away.

The sun attempted to make amends now for the morning's rain, and its warmth - strained through several layers of cloud - was sufficient to set the grass steaming way below. Yet through the shimmering veil of rain-in-reverse we could see to the southern end of the Lac de Neuchâtel, and a thousand green pastures folded neatly and laid out to dry.

The path leads easily up the green slope of ridge to the summit crown of **LE CHASSERON** (1,607m 5 hours) where there is an extensive panorama overlooking the Mittelland and out to the Alps, while on the western side the mountain drops steeply in limestone cliffs. From the summit the route now descends south for a short distance to reach a hotel.

HOTEL du CHASSERON (1,589m *Restaurant. Accommodation in bedrooms and touristenlager.*)

The path wanders back to the ridge (almost an escarpment again) and continues along the very edge beside a fence. It's an undulating ridge with interesting views, and along the way you will pass a transmitter tower and a ski tow. Then at last waymarks lead down through pastures to **LES AVATTES** (1,458m *Refreshments*) at the head of

84

several ski tows. The path descends below the restaurant, then swings to the right beneath the tows, into another pasture and joins a clear track which leads all the way down to Sainte-Croix.

(1) **SAINTE-CROIX** (1,066m 6 hours 30 mins) *Hotels, Youth Hostel, Restaurants. All services. Shops, banks, PTT. Postbuses, railway. Tourist Information Office.*

*   *   *

Places Visited on the Way
1. *Sainte-Croix:* This is a pleasant little town set in a hollow between Le Chasseron and Mont de Baulmes. Well-geared for tourists - other than Neuchâtel, the first to do so along the JHR. It's a fine centre for cross-country skiing, which means that accommodation to be found here will be equally suitable for the long-distance walker in summer (drying rooms etc.). A good assortment of shops and a very helpful staff in the Tourist Information Office. Sainte-Croix is home of the musical box industry, and there's a local museum displaying samples of the craft.

*   *   *

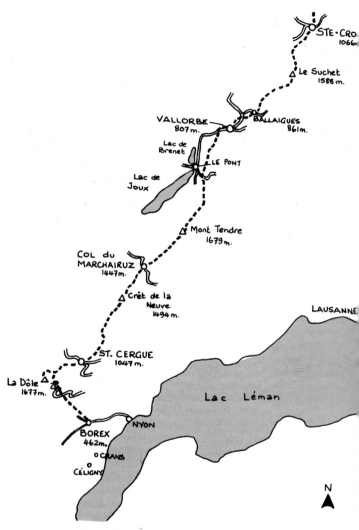

STE·CRO
1066

Le Suchet
1588 m.

VALLORBE
807 m.

BALLAIGUES
861m.

Lac de
Brenet

LE PONT

Lac de
Joux

Mont Tendre
1679 m.

COL du
MARCHAIRUZ
1447m.

Crêt de la
Neuve
1494 m.

LAUSANNE

ST. CERGUE
1047 m.

La Dôle
1677m.

Lac Léman

BOREX
462m.

NYON

CRANS

CÉLIGNY

N

JURA HIGH ROUTE: STAGES 11-14

STAGE 11:
SAINTE-CROIX-LE SUCHET-VALLORBE

Distance:	22.5 kilometres
Time	6 hours
Start altitude:	1,066m High point: Le Suchet 1,588m
Maps:	L.S. 241 Val de Travers 1:50,000
	L.S. 5020 Yverdon-les-Bains-Lausanne 1:50,000
	K & F 5 Yverdon, Ste-Croix-Val de Travers
	1:50,000
Accommodation:	Vallorbe - Hotels, Youth Hostel, Campsite
	And elsewhere along the route. (See text)

*The summit of Le Suchet is the physical and literal highpoint of this Stage.
It gives an almost 360° panorama which includes the Alps, the Mittelland
and a large portion of the main Jura ridge. But there are many other
pleasures to enjoy along the way too.*

*Initially there is a steady climb out of Sainte-Croix which leads to a long
open plateau close to the French border; a tranquil landscape, not dramatic
but lush and pleasant, an unhurried land to amble slowly through. There
are plenty of signs of military defences - a reminder of Switzerland's vulner-
ability in times of war, and its land-locked isolation when the rest of Europe
was twice before this century gripped in battle. These defences make a
curious focus of interest, incongruous though they may seem in this land of
flower meadows and cowbells.*

*The Aiguilles de Baulmes look down on mellow pastures as the route
approaches the sharp climb up to Le Suchet. Then, southward beyond the
high ridge, the descent goes among meadows and a patch of forest, passing
farms and attractive houses, and enters the village of Ballaigues. From
there to Vallorbe is a devious route to avoid a modern road which passes
through the valley. And then to Vallorbe itself, a small town on an
important international railway, but with a heart that is quite delightful.*

*As with the previous Stage there are times when parts of this route
between Grange Neuve and Le Suchet are affected by military exercises.
Check with the Tourist Information Office in Sainte-Croix, or by writing
in advance to the address given at the head of Stage 10.*

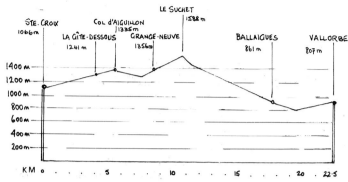

PROFILE: STAGE 11 STE. CROIX - VALLORBE

There are no water supplies until you reach Ballaigues, 5 hours from Sainte-Croix, but there are several refreshment possibilities along the way. Fill water bottles before setting out.

*   *   *

Waymarks through Sainte-Croix lead the route down to the railway station and back into town once more. Unless you need to visit the station, walk along Rue Centrale (the main shopping street by which you entered) heading north-west, then bear right into Rue de France, which is waymarked *Chemin des Crêtes*. This leads you climbing above the town, and a footpath then heads up a sloping pasture. A winding trail leads to a narrow road, and from there you take a waymarked track heading past a house. It takes you through a patch of forest, across pastures and among woodlands again, happily on an easy gradient now after the climb out of Sainte-Croix.

The track leads through many pleasant meadows, passes some military defences (the French border is only 3 kilometres away to the west) and comes to the little hamlet of **LA GÎTE DESSOUS** (1,241m 1 hour 10 mins. *Refreshments*) which consists of a few farms and a restaurant.

Follow the narrow country road through the village and on for about 3 kilometres. It takes you through open meadowland, past one or two farms, onto a broad green plateau with forested hills to the south and the east, and far views to the west over a panorama of low hills that run into France, and back to the north-east to the heights over which the route came yesterday. A peaceful, soft land.

The road crosses a slight rise in woodlands at the **COL de l'AIGUILLON** (1,335m 1 hour 45 mins), then slopes down again through more military defences. (Note the white limestone cliffs of the so-called **Aiguilles de Baulmes** rising above to the left.)

Shortly after coming out of the woods break away from the road on a waymarked path slanting down through pastures to the right, then go through a gap in a drystone wall and up the slope beyond towards a small building. Continue over pastures and swing up towards some trees to the right of a track, still following waymarks and on a narrow path. For a while this path goes along a line of telegraph poles and up a grassy dome of a hill. But before reaching the hill's summit you must traverse along its left-hand slope, then lose a little height to reach the farm/restaurant of Grange Neuve.

GRANGE NEUVE (1,356m 2 hours 25 mins   *Refreshments. Tourist-enlager accommodation.*)

Grange Neuve overlooks a lovely bowl of pasture with the steep rise of Le Suchet opposite. Knowing we would soon have to face a stiff climb we easily gave in to the temptation for a Sinalco stop, and sat there in the morning sunshine while a local farmer swung his long-handled scythe nearby, cutting a minor forest of dock. The sweat gleamed on his face and arms while we allowed ours to dry. Yesterday, I remembered, there'd been little to make us sweat other than the weight of the rucksacks on our backs. Today a bright sky reminded us that this was summer. We welcomed its return.

I went inside the farm/restaurant to inspect the plumbing and followed signs marked WC. Opening a door I found myself in the cattle byre where about fifty cows waited to be milked, patiently standing or lying in their stalls chewing at the straw, adding to the slurry on the floor. It was a fragrant, unquiet place with the sounds of chewing and lowing and bovine belching, and it proved to be the most public toilet in the whole Jura.

The waymarked path/track crosses the pastureland to the south of Grange Neuve, and traverses the hill slope with a fine view to enjoy down a scoop of hillside to the ridges and forests of France, little more than a kilometre away now. The track narrows to a slender path in forest where it begins to climb steeply emerging to a broad grassland with the triangulation marker of Le Suchet's summit seen to the left. Although it is not necessary to go to the summit, it is well worth visiting for its huge panorama, and takes little more than about five minutes to reach from here.

(1)   **LE SUCHET** (1,588m 3 hours 10 mins)

To continue the High Route cross ahead over the grassy saddle heading east, now with a huge view before you, and descend a little on the far side to reach another farm/restaurant, Chalet du Suchet.

CHALET du SUCHET (1,489m 3 hours 25 mins *Refreshments. Touristenlager accommodation*)
Bear right along a track at the farm, then veer left where the track forks. It's only a grassy trail, but there are a few waymarks on rocks, and it now heads south-west across yet more pastures. The trail becomes a clear path that descends among trees and through yet more lovely flower meadows to another farm, **LA POYETTE** (1,331m), set in the midst of a veritable wall of military defences. Continue ahead towards an enclosed patch of forest that you pass to your right, and enter a long meadow almost totally surrounded by forest. You will come to a lone farm building, cross a narrow road and continue ahead. At the end of the meadow enter a forest on a clear path that soon comes to a track near yet another farm, this one off to your right, **LA LANGUETINE** (1,217m).

Bear right and pass the farm to find a trail that soon becomes a track going through forest. A few metres before the forest ends veer half-left along a narrow waymarked path that drops down to a country road where you turn right. On coming to crossroads at **LA BESSONE** (1,090m) go straight ahead and pass to the left of a farm, and then follow a track across a large open area of agricultural land with expansive views that stretch as far as the lake of Geneva.

On the far side of the fields the track slopes down among trees, then beside lovely pastures, and eventually joins another country road. Follow along this, guided by waymarks for short-cuts, all the way to the village of Ballaigues.

BALLAIGUES (861m 4 hours 50 mins *Hotels. Restaurant. Food shops, PTT, water supply. Public toilets. Postbus (to Vallorbe).*)
Bear right and walk through the village along the main street, and on coming to the western outskirts veer left down a tarmac path and onto a narrow road which takes you across the main valley highway. 100 metres later bear right along a track which leads to a forest road. Follow this through a stretch of forest then, guided by waymarks, you will come to the **BARRAGE de la JOUGNENA** (793m) that has dammed the River La Jougnena in a narrowing of valley. Cross the barrage and come to a main road. Go over this and follow a minor road ahead all the way to Vallorbe railway station overlooking the town.

(2) **VALLORBE** (807m 6 hours) *Hotels, Youth Hostel, Campsite. Restaurants, shops, banks, PTT. All services. Tourist Information Office. Railway (TGV to Paris and Lausanne) Postbuses.*

* * *

Places Seen on the Way

1. *Le Suchet:* This prominent summit gives an amazing, near 360° panorama. It overlooks the Mittelland and the Alps, the Lac de Neuchâtel and the crest of the Jura stretching from Chasseral in the north, to La Dôle in the south-west. Since the French border lies only one kilometre to the west, and the western Jura is comparatively low-lying, the panorama includes a huge portion of green French countryside too. Le Suchet is justifiably famous in this corner of the Jura for its views, and there will invariably be others to share the summit with you.

2. *Vallorbe:* A bustling small town, it has a most attractive heart where the River Orbe flows through, passing some fine, interesting buildings. There has been a forge here since 1495, and a museum has now been installed in the same building. With its main-line rail access, Vallorbe has a few local industries, but tourism clearly forms an important part of its economy. A short distance from the town, and on the route of Stage 12, is the picturesque Source de l'Orbe, where numerous clear streams come gushing through the woods to unite into the one main river. The Orbe is, in fact, the resurgence of an outflow from Lac Brenet.

* * *

STAGE 12:
VALLORBE-MONT TENDRE-COL du MARCHAIRUZ

Distance:	30.5 kilometres
Time:	8 hours 30 mins
Start altitude:	807m High point: Mont Tendre 1,679m
Maps:	L.S. 5020 Yverdon-les-Bains-Lausanne 1:50,000
	K & F 6 Lausanne-La Côte,
	St. Cergue-Vallée de Joux 1:50,000
Accommodation:	Col du Marchairuz - Hotel
	And vague possibility elsewhere along the route.
	(See text)

The longest Stage of the High Route, it is demanding through limitations of accommodation along the way. Some choose to break it by having a short (2 hours 40 mins) stroll to Le Pont on the promontory between the Lacs de Joux and Brenet where there are hotels, thus giving a second day of 5 hours 50 minutes. There is much to argue in favour of this plan, since Le Pont is in such an attractive position, and a rest day will not come amiss at this point in the walk, given sufficient time. However, the long walk over Mont Tendre to Col du Marchairuz will not be too daunting for walkers who have survived the route thus far. There is a CAS hut (Refuge du Cunay) to the south-west of Mont Tendre, but it is not normally open except at weekends, unless members are in occupation mid-week when it may be possible to claim an overnight's lodging.

The route from Vallorbe first visits the Source de l'Orbe, then cuts back before heading up through forest on a long winding track, through a funnel of hill-squeezed valley and out to pastures above Le Pont. Without descending to the unseen lakeside the JHR crosses through a series of meadows on a long approach to the highest point of the Swiss Jura, Mont Tendre, more than six hours after leaving Vallorbe.

From the ridge there are lovely views into the Vallée de Joux and over a lush folding landscape, all green and pastoral and welcoming. Then the path descends from the ridge, only to regain it a little farther to the south-

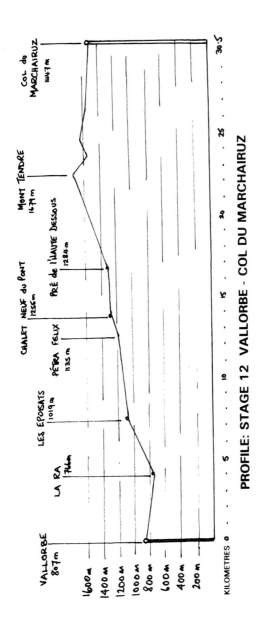

PROFILE: STAGE 12 VALLORBE - COL DU MARCHAIRUZ

93

west where it skirts Grand Cunay for some of the finest walking of the whole Jura. It is then a short stroll to the road pass of Col du Marchairuz and the hotel with its bedrooms and touristenlager accommodation.

There are one or two water sources along the route, but these are located in the early part of the walk, and there is only one opportunity to buy liquid refreshment later (a few metres below the summit of Mont Tendre).

As with the two previous Stages, this area is sometimes used for military exercises. (See notes at the head of Stage 10.) For advance information write to: Waffenplatzcommando, CH 1140 Bière, or telephone: 021/77 53 51. Warning should also be given against handling any strange pieces of metal you might find lying about. Shells are sometimes used during training exercises, and although every effort is made by the authorities to collect expended material, some may be missed. Do not touch anything which might be a shell, or part of one. Make a note of its position, and tell someone when you arrive at either a farm or the hotel at the end of the day.

That having been said, do not be alarmed by the above notes. You may be unfortunate in having to re-route this Stage (or, time willing, you could rest for a day in Le Pont until the exercises are over), but mostly, of course, you will wander along the route without any difficulty or delay. It is indeed a very fine day's outing to enjoy to the fullest.

* * *

From Vallorbe railway station the route heads west along a signposted narrow road towards the Source de l'Orbe. It soon slopes downhill on a hard-surfaced path (signpost directing to the Grottes) to some houses, where you bear right along a road. After passing a line of terraced houses the road forks. Take the left branch and a few paces later go half-left again down a sloping track among trees. This brings you to another road and you continue ahead in the same direction. On coming to the **CAFÉ de la SOURCE** *(Refreshments)* the road forks and you take the right branch. (Water supply nearby.)

The road narrows, swings left and descends a little, and continues on a most attractive course among trees crossing one stream after another - the **SOURCE de la ORBE** (780m 40 mins). When you come to a footbridge on the left spanning the main River Orbe, cross over and join a broad track where you turn left. *(For refreshments, turn right for a few paces to a restaurant.)* Now virtually doubling-back on the approach route, follow the track which soon becomes a surfaced road.

Leave the woods and pass beside a large hydro-electricity works. Continue ahead, soon with pastures alongside. (You will see a path heading to the right which is signposted to Le Pont, but this is not our route although it joins the main JHR later.) After about 1 kilometre of this road you bear right on a waymarked track to pass a farm, **LA RA** (766m *Water supply outside*).

The track now climbs into forest, winding through and gaining height over about 1.5 kilometres, until at last you emerge through a long flowery meadow section narrowed by the constricting walls of the hills. Continue along the track and cross a railway line at a point known as **LES EPOISATS** (1,019m 2 hours) where the railway disappears into a tunnel. Still following the track ahead you continue to gain height through this narrow valley until it opens to a large meadowland where the track forks. (Water source here.)

Note: For those planning to visit Le PONT (1,008m - in another 20 mins - total 2 hours 40 mins from Vallorbe; Hotels, refreshments, railway, Postbus) take the right branch and follow all the way to the village which is set most attractively between two lakes.

For the main JHR to Mont Tendre and Col du Marchairuz, take the left branch and follow ahead along the track. About 250 metres later bear left on a small path going uphill, and soon rejoin the track that has made a long loop round. The track forks again. Bear right and right again a few paces later and walk along the track through pastures. When the track swings to the right, bear left to go through a gateway and ahead over more pastures towards a stretch of forest. After about 250 metres from the gateway bear right to gain a wide road (Le Pont-Col du Mollendruz) at **PÉTRA FÉLIX** (1,135m). Cross to a minor road opposite. *(If there are to be military exercises taking place, there will almost certainly be notices posted here.)*

Wander ahead along this road which takes you through a pleasant region of pastures, and soon you will gain a view to the right down to the Lacs de Joux and Brenet with the little village of Le Pont spread on the strip of land separating the two.

Continue along the road, winding among grassy meadows and trees, until you see a farm ahead with a rough track leading to it. Take the track and pass the farm towards woods. The route leads through these and out the other side among more pastures, now on a narrow surfaced road. After about 250 metres or so veer left up rough pastures along a vague grassy trail which goes about 50 metres from the forest edge. (It is merely a short cut to avoid a loop in the road.) You regain the road once more and follow along it to a gateway with a rough track leading off half-left ahead. Walk along this until it forks, then bear right for a few paces before cutting off along a grassy path half-left. There is a shortage of waymarks, but the path is clear enough; a grassy pathway leading among open glades and over an undulating, flower-bright, almost moorland area. It is a delightful stretch of country, with hills rising in the south that lead up to Mont Tendre.

The path brings you into a large open bowl of pastureland with a couple of farms in it, and a narrow road crossing at the far side. This is **PRÉ de l'HAUTE DESSOUS** (1,284m 4 hours 30 mins).

When you reach the narrow road bear right and walk along it (now a track) to pass a farm seen off to your left. The track leads among trees and pastures for about 1.5 kilometres, then you bear left up a grassy slope which is waymarked, and into forest on a clear path. On emerging soon after, go up another grassy slope, then bear right along a fairly level course following a narrow path with a few waymarks.

At the end of the level section of path, it swings left and climbs more grass slopes to reach a solitary farm, **CHALET de PIERRE** (1,551m) occupying a balcony site overlooking a broad view of the Vallée de Joux and the French hills beyond. Here you join a broad track heading to the left and follow it curving uphill on an easy gradient, soon to reach another farm offering refreshments; **CHALET du MONT TENDRE** (1,646m 6 hours 10 mins. *Refreshments*) from which there is a clear view to the south-west where Mont Tendre's large triangulation point signals the summit about 500 metres away.

The path continues towards the summit showing the folding limestone strata quite clearly, and soon gains it without difficulty.

(1) **MONT TENDRE** (1,679m 6 hours 25 mins.)
As the highest point in the Swiss Jura the summit is perhaps a little disappointing, for it offers no dramatic peak, but rather little more than one more rise along the ridge. But the views are splendid, and it is worth resting awhile here to enjoy them before descending on the south-western ridge-slope to a signpost that directs the JHR to the right, through a drystone wall, and down grassy slopes towards a farm. This is **CHALET de YENS** (1,589m).

Pass alongside this and continue beyond through a gentle trough of hillside heading towards the south-west, through another wall and along a vague grassy path. This path becomes a little more obvious, loses some height, then begins to regain that height once more, winding steadily upwards among trees. Then you come to yet another drystone wall beyond which you will see a building ahead on the ridge.

Note: **REFUGE du CUNAY** *(1,567m 7 hours 40 mins, 30 places in dormitories) will be found a little to the left of this building, about 150 metres from the path across a stretch of pasture.*

We were fortunate, the hut was open and occupied by a Swiss family and a group of four Dutchmen - one of whom was a member of the Vallée de

Mont Tendre's ridge - looking north (Chalet du Mont Tendre seen below ridge on right).

Joux section of the CAS that owned the refuge. He often travelled all the way from Holland to spend a weekend here, and was a true enthusiast of the Jura, and especially of this hut. I could well understand his enthusiasm, for it certainly was a splendid place; warm, comfortable, well-equipped and in an idyllic situation. And that night when the weather again turned disagreeable I lay in the dormitory listening to the howling of the wind and the torrential rain beating onto the balcony, and felt well-satisfied to be here. But in the morning a miracle had occurred, for a transformation had taken place. Gone were the rainclouds, and instead we were greeted by one of those sparkling mountain mornings when the sky showed undisguised promise and the only clouds were those that lay below, spread in a blanket of white in every valley, with just the green hilltops showing through. Refuge du Cunay smiled in the early morning sun as it gazed over a world that was lost in its ignorance of the glory that was ours.

Regain the ridge path above the hut and continue in a southwesterly direction, soon dropping down to join a narrow service road where you bear right. After a short distance head left to make a short cut across a piece of pastureland to avoid a wide loop of the road, and briefly rejoining it you soon break away once more to the left across sloping pastures with pleasant views all around. On joining a grassy

Cattle near Grand Cunay, south of Mont Tendre.

track you veer to the left again and follow as it rises among trees and goes up onto a hillock where there is a wonderful panoramic view of the rolling green Jura country, and down into a bowl of pastureland to the south where a number of farms are situated.

There were cows grazing on the hilltop, their bells clattering in the champagne-like air. Apart from them we had the world to ourselves, and I gazed at the country spread below and attempted to absorb the moment. It certainly was a glorious patch of country. It had no wild-mountain drama, no soaring peaks nor savage valleys. There were no lakes to gleam in the sunlight, nor rivers full of crash and roar. This was a soft and gentle landscape; a vast expanse of greenery checked here and there with a strip of white limestone wall dividing one man's land from another's. There were fluffs of cream far-off in distant valleys. There were finches piping in the nearest trees and a tiny speck circling way, way above us that was undoubtedly a bird of prey mocking us with the power of flight. There were tiny flowers crammed in the exposed rocks of the hilltop, and taller plants wavering in the grass. And I knew then the splendour of the Jura, and wished to be nowhere else. All the mountains of other ranges had their magic that would draw me back to them in time. But so too had the modest hills of the Jura. This was country to hold onto. A moment to savour for itself.

Now following a few waymarks pass along the left-hand side of the sloping limestone-and-turf crest, beyond a solitary farm building and down to the foot of the slope to pass another hut, and go up the opposite hillside along a grassy trail. The track now leads over a hillock and down to another farm, **MONTS de BIÈRE DERRIÈRE** (1,481m 8 hours).

Pass along the left-hand side of this farm and into the pasture beyond, then curve away to the right along a waymarked track. This narrows to a path climbing then falling among trees and a lush vegetation. It broadens once more to a track which leads directly to Col du Marchairuz with its large hotel/restaurant beside the road.

COL du MARCHAIRUZ (1,447m 8 hours 30 mins.   *Refreshments. Hotel with beds (6) and touristenlager accommodation (35 places). Postbuses (summer only) north to Le Brassus (hotels, touristenlager), and south to St. George (touristenlager).)*

*   *   *

Places Visited on the Way
1. *Mont Tendre:* The highest summit of the Swiss Jura (1,679m -two metres higher than La Dôle), it overlooks the Vallée de Joux and the French Jura as far north as the Vosges. Southwards, beyond the lesser Jura ridges, the view stretches over Lac Léman (the lake of Geneva) to the Alps. A very large metal triangulation marker adorns the summit.

*   *   *

STAGE 13:
COL du MARCHAIRUZ-CRÊT de la NEUVE-ST. CERGUE

Distance: 16.5 kilometres
Time: 4 hours 30 mins
Start altitude: 1,447m   High point: Crêt de la Neuve 1,494m
Maps: L.S. 260 St. Cergue 1:50,000
                   K & F 6 Lausanne-La Côte,
                   St. Cergue-Vallée de Joux 1:50,000
Accommodation: St. Cergue - Hotels, Youth Hostel, Campsite

Perhaps the first point to make with regard to this penultimate Stage of the High Route is that water bottles should be filled before setting out. There are no opportunities to replenish supplies along the way, and no cafés or restaurants either. A dry Stage, but a short Stage.

Throughout the day there are isolated farms set amid hilly pastures. But there are also forested sections opening now and then to distant views of Lac Léman shimmering in the south-east, and snow-capped peaks beyond. The Alps are drawing nearer with every day. Waymarking is a little sparse at times and on occasion the path becomes very faint among the pastures, but there should be no real route-finding difficulties as, with a moment's concentration, the way will become obvious.

As on a few recent Stages, there are periods when military exercises affect a part of the route between Marchairuz and St. Cergue. See notes at the head of Stages 10 and 12 for details.

*   *   *

Pass along the car park side of the Hotel du Marchairuz and find a narrow path beyond, leading among trees and a full and lush vegetation. It brings you down to a long, narrow meadowland with forest rising to the left. The path heads through the centre of this meadowland, down to a dip and up then to a grassy saddle. A second saddle lies ahead, and after reaching this the route slopes into a broader pasture and joins a clear track. Continue straight ahead along this

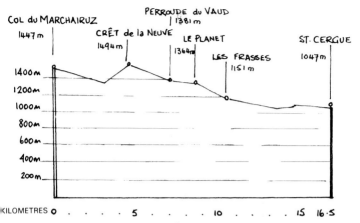

PROFILE: STAGE 13 COL DU MARCHAIRUZ - ST. CERGUE

track. As it begins to wind to the left a signpost directs the *Chemin des Crêtes* onto a path heading half-right and down into a continuing meadowland.

The path wanders through undulating pastures for some way, and then rises up a slope to a small solitary farm, **La NEUVE** (1,444m 1 hour 10 mins). Now bear left along a narrow roadway for a few paces, but when it swings to the left, leave it and go straight ahead up a short slope on a waymarked path among trees to reach a limestone hummock bearing a large cross. This is **CRÊT de la NEUVE** (1,494m 1 hour 20 mins).

This bluff of limestone and turf bore a profusion of wild flowers. There were martagon lilies to one side, mixed with a few specimens of the black vanilla orchid (Nigritella nigra). There were matted cushions of androsace exploiting otherwise bare terraces of rock, and tiny blue stars of the snow gentian (Gentiana nivalis) growing on the crown of the hill and down its slopes. Some of the plants were extravagant show pieces; others were modest, attempting to conceal their beauty among the rocks or long grass that grew nearby. All around there was colour. There were far views to the south too, from the grassy bluff opposite the cross. We were seduced by the natural world and happily stopped there for quite some time enjoying the quiet wonder of the place, with only the song of birds among the trees and crickets buzzing in the grass for company, before conscience took over and we set off again along the faint path.

101

*Campanulas clustered among the rocks of the
Crêt de la Neuve.*

The vague grassy trail continues beyond the Crêt de la Neuve and its large cross, then bears left a little to become a more obvious path which leads among trees. After a while the path comes onto a track leading to a farm called **PERROUDE de MARCHISSY** (1,429m) and there you continue ahead on a signposted route. A faint grassy path leads once more through pastureland, winds over an open glade and among trees, then goes half-right down to a spacious pastureland with forest skirting it. Waymarks lead across this and join another track at a signpost. You then bear left among trees and cross more pastures to yet another farm standing off to the left; **PERROUDE du VAUD** (1,381m 2 hours). A few metres beyond the farm the route comes to a narrow surfaced road where you turn left.

Follow the road for about 400 metres as it winds among trees, then when it makes a determined left-hand sweep, break away from it to the right along a waymarked grassy path leading uphill through a wedge of pastureland. The way leads among meadows to another isolated farm, **Le PLANET** (1,364m 2 hours 25 mins), and a few paces after this bear left (another magnificent flower meadow) towards woods and onto a clear path heading south. Following this path, cross a patch of meadowland and re-enter the woods where you bear right.

The trail leads downhill through the woods, and on coming to cross-paths you continue straight ahead.

When you come to a narrow road cross directly over and continue the descent through the woodlands, now quite steeply, and eventually emerge into a narrow patch of sloping pasture. Walk ahead, then swing right and left through more pastures where you will come to one more farm, **Les FRASSES** (1,151m 2 hours 55 mins).

Continue past the farm and down a rough track. On coming to crosstracks go straight over, now following ahead towards a forest. Having crossed a meadowland you then enter the forest *(Bois d'Oujon)* and continue ahead, now and then catching fragmentary views across to the lake of Geneva. When you reach a narrow road go straight ahead and continue along the forest track, so to reach the ruins of a 12th century convent, **RUINES d'OUJON** (1,040m 3 hours 35 mins), seen to the right in a rough opening.

On the far side of the opening, beyond the ruins, continue along the forest track as it bears left. This winds on, still through trees, then you veer right on a narrow grassy path which is both signposted and waymarked. It will bring you out of the forest to cross a narrow road, then straight ahead along a surfaced farm road which works its way through open pastureland and fields and past a couple of farms with big views left towards Lac Léman and the Alps.

About 150 metres beyond the second farm bear right along a grassy trail leading towards more woods. Entering these a narrow path takes you ahead, then out across open undulating pastures with views ahead to the rising hills that congregate around La Dôle. These pastures, heavy with flowers and shrubs, lead onto a narrow country road where you bear left. After something like 80 metres, head to the right on a track that is signposted to St. Cergue Gare (station).

On joining a road turn left and walk down into the village of St. Cergue which you enter near the railway station.

(1) **ST. CERGUE** (1047m 4 hours 30 mins) *Hotels, Youth Hostel, Campsite. Restaurants, shops, banks, PTT. Railway (to Nyon). Tourist Information Office.*

* * *

Places Visited on the Way
1. *St. Cergue:* An attractive village built on slopes overlooking Lac Léman and the Alps, it has become popular as both a summer and winter sports resort without compromising its charm. With La Dôle

103

rising to the south-west and a vast area of pasture and forest on either side, the village boasts walks that open to a 300km. panorama of the Alps stretching from the Jungfrau to Mont Blanc; a view which Thomas Arnold 'never saw surpassed'. In winter there are downhill skiing facilities (Ski school, tow etc.) and 50 kilometres of maintained cross-country pistes.

*   *   *

Great Yellow Gentian

STAGE 14:
ST. CERGUE-LA DÔLE-BOREX

Distance: 18.5 kilometres
Time: 5 hours 40 mins
Start altitude: 1,047m   High point: La Dôle 1,677m
Maps: L.S. 260 St. Cergue 1:50,000
                     K & F 6 Lausanne-La Côte,
                     St. Cergue-Vallée de Joux 1:50,000
Accommodation: None

This, the final Stage of the High Route, gives a day of contrasting views and a fair mixture of countryside to wander through. It has its moments of easy walking, but there are also some taxing stretches leading to the cluttered summit of La Dôle, and similarly on the long descent through the pastures and forests that lead to the low farmland spreading from the foot of the Jura hills to Borex.

Of all the High Route sections this is likely to be the one on which solitude is least of all to be experienced. La Dôle has a certain mystique about it - some authorities mistakenly claim it to be the highest summit in the Swiss Jura - and it gives a much-lauded view. And since one can drive to within 45 minutes of the top, there will invariably be many walkers making the ascent during the summer.

The high point of the walk comes early in the day - after less than two and a half hours from St. Cergue, and thereafter one faces a descent of almost twelve hundred metres to the lowlands. It's an interesting walk.

Again, there are rare instances when this section will be affected by military training exercises. Check with the local Tourist Information Office in St. Cergue prior to setting out, or telephone the area command on: 021/77 53 51 (Mon-Fri 07.00-11.45 and 13.00-17.00).

Water bottles should be filled on departure, as the first opportunity to refill does not come for several hours and there are no cafés or restaurants before Borex.

* * *

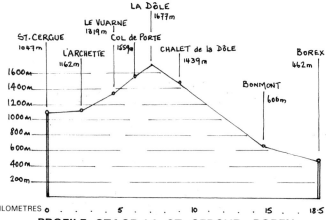

PROFILE: STAGE 14 ST. CERGUE - BOREX

Immediately before reaching the railway station on entering St. Cergue, take the road heading off to the right and follow through the village (waymarks on posts), passing the Youth Hostel on the way. Then, near the southern end of St. Cergue, bear right along a side street with the JHR signpost directing to Le Vuarne, La Dôle and Borex. It's a short street which leads onto a track passing tennis courts. Just beyond these the track forks. Continue ahead between trees, and the track then takes you to a narrow surfaced road where you bear left. On coming to a broad junction of roads continue straight ahead to pass the village campsite on your right. About 100 metres beyond this, leave the road in favour of a path heading half-left (parallel with the road) through pastureland towards a collection of chalets on the hillside ahead.

In the far left-hand corner of the pasture join a track which soon comes to a road. Shortly after this break off to the left on a signposted route, then left again on another road. This soon forks. Take the left branch with a large transmitter mast seen ahead on the ridge above forest slopes. The road ends by a chair-lift station, **L'ARCHETTE** (1,162m 40 mins), and the continuing path is reached through a gate to the right of the car parking area.

This clear path takes you up a long narrow grass slope heading south rather steeply. Halfway up the slope you cross a narrow roadway and continue straight ahead until you come to a second road. Here you turn right and follow along this road for almost a kilometre.

106

Walkers at Col de Porte below La Dôle.

When the narrow road makes a sudden right-hand curve to reach a farm, known as **Le VUARNE** (1,319m 1 hour 15 mins), leave it and go straight ahead on a continuing track leading through a narrow valley of pasture heading south-west. At the head of the pasture a path climbs among trees, crosses a track and goes straight up a steep gully. Coming over hilly pastures at the head of the gully you gain a clear view ahead of La Dôle, with its limestone strata clearly exposed on the east face of the mountain, and a great radar dome dominating the summit.

The path continues over pastures, then passes a hut on the right belonging to the Nyon Ski Club, and comes to a crossing path at **COL de PORTE** (1,559m 2 hours). Ahead lies the route to the summit of La Dôle. To the left the path drops steeply toward the Chalet de la Dôle and on to Borex, while to the right a narrow trail decends to the north to Col de la Givrine and France.

Although for the continuation of the JHR it is not necessary to walk up to the summit of La Dôle, it is worth leaving rucksacks here and making the twenty minute ascent before turning your back on the Jura and descending to the foothills.

The ascent path is a clear one which goes round to the western side of the ridge, passes an area of ski tows, and then regains the crest (bright with wild flowers) for the final stretch to the summit.

(1) **La DÔLE** (1,677m 2 hours 20 mins)

The views are supposed to be vast from the summit. 'The moment when from the top of the Jura mountains I discovered Lake Geneva, was a moment of ecstasy and delight', wrote Rousseau. We, however, had to content ourselves with imagining a vista of Mont Blanc and the great array of snowpeaks and glacial-clad Alpine giants, for our vision was blinkered by banks of cloud. Instead we gazed into valleys far below green with pasture, gold with a harvest of wheat, almost black with forest, and a hint of Lac Léman. But no great snow giants to take our minds from the horror story of man's technological marvels cluttering the dome of a summit.

We looked along the continuing green ridge that headed into those clouds, and knew that France was not far off. Our Jura ridge walk across Switzerland was all but over. Yet off to the south-west the hills still had a long way to go, and there were other peaks, other valleys, other flowers and hawks and distant views and challenging horizons waiting. Maybe for a winter season? On ski? Turning to the north we began to retrace our steps to the col, and as we did so we caught sight of the familiar Jura ridges we had wandered during the past several days. We recognised patches of meadow, the shape of forests, the rise of a prominent hill and knew a curious pride in that recognition. In that warm pride of familiarity we knew we would take the Jura with us, down to the lowlands and all the way home.

Return to the Col de Porte and take the path heading south, quite steeply at first among a few trees and shrubs, to the rough pastures in which sits the large **CHALET de la DÔLE** (1,439m 2 hours 50 mins). The path leads to a surfaced road beside the chalet. Walk left along this heading south-east for about 500 metres until you come to forest and a junction of roads.

Waymarks direct the route ahead now onto a path that cuts through the forest, steeply down at times, for about 4 kilometres or so. It is a narrow path in places; a track in others, and it crosses and recrosses the winding road several times. On coming to a clear forest track it leads to a hut, **Le BAULOZ** (1,137m 3 hours 35 mins), where there is a water supply nearby - the first since St. Cergue. The track leads onto the road again which you follow for a while until you come to a hairpin bend where a signpost directs the continuing path off to the right. This descends quite steeply still in the forest.

Again you come to road, then onto a footpath again with the sound of a stream off to the right; then once more to a road where you go to the right. Again waymarks take our route onto a footpath on the left

108

among the trees for the final stretch of forest that brings you onto the road at **BONMONT** (606m 4 hours 40 mins). Continue down the road for a few hundred metres until a signpost directs the continuing *Chemin des Crêtes* to the left along a footpath among trees. Out of these and onto a track where you bear left and follow for about 150 metres until you come to a road bearing right. Along this you leave the shade of trees, and are faced with the lake of Geneva (Lac Léman) ahead and mountains of the Alps on the far side.

Suddenly you are out of the Jura hills and among flat farmlands. The hills continue to roll away behind you, but ahead stretches the road that can only take you from them.

It was now a very different world; a lowland agricultural plain with barely a rise between us and the lake, several kilometres away, and the sun beat down upon us. Fat heads of grain were popping under the sun's heat in the cornfield on our left, and a combined harvester rumbled through a large field off to our right. Skylarks trilled high above; mere specks in a huge open sky of blue. Out of the hills and into the plain. From grassy ridges to tarmac beneath our boots. From forest to cornfield. The Jura slipped away.

Walk straight ahead along the quiet country road with your back to the hills for about 3 kilometres, until you come to a crossroads where a signpost leads you straight over, through more farmland, towards Lac Léman and the village of Borex.

Borex sits at a crossroads. The end of the Jura High Route with an attractive water trough (non-drinkable) a few metres from the Post Office. Behind stretch some 299 kilometres of hill and forest, of pasture and broad vista. And a host of memories...

(2) **BOREX** (462m 5 hours 40 mins) *Restaurant, PTT, Postbus (to Nyon).*

* * *

Routes Out of Borex
a) Take the Postbus (infrequent) to Nyon for mainline trains to Geneva - or trains from Nyon to Lausanne for a direct route to Paris (including TGV).
b) Walk about 6 kilometres (via Arnex - signpost at water trough in Borex) to either Crans or Céligny (Hotel) for local trains to Geneva.

Places Visited on the Way
1. *La Dôle:* The western-most summit of the Swiss Jura chain and

second in height after Mont Tendre, the summit view is extensive and supposedly includes Mont Blanc and the big peaks of the Oberland, as well as a considerable portion of the Jura. Apparently the view is best seen in the afternoon. The summit itself is adorned with a huge radome (radar dish encased in a golf ball protective envelope) and various items of meteorological equipment - the most cluttered summit of the author's career! But the wild flowers on the ridge approaching are a fine representative collection of limestone-loving alpines.

2. *Borex:* Marking the conclusion of the Jura High Route, Borex is a small, tidy farming village built on a crossroads about 7 kilometres west of Nyon, between the Jura hills and Lac Léman. In the main square stands an attractive 16th century house near the water trough. On the northern edge of the village a new housing development is the walker's first sign of Borex. The original village has more appeal.

*   *   *

St.Cergue Youth Hostel

110

SUMMARY TABLE OF ROUTE AND TIMINGS
FOR THE JURA HÖHENWEG

Stage 1: **Dielsdorf to Brugg** (23 kilometres)
429m	Dielsdorf	
385m	Baden	4 hours
352m	Brugg	6 hours 50 mins

Stage 2: **Brugg to Staffelegg** (15.5 kilometres)
352m	Brugg	
722m	Linnerberg	2 hours 25 mins
621m	Staffelegg	4 hours 10 mins

Stage 3: **Staffelegg to Hauenstein** (20.5 kilometres)
621m	Staffelegg	
963m	Geissflue	3 hours 25 mins
674m	Hauenstein	6 hours

Stage 4: **Hauenstein to Balsthal** (20.5 kilometres)
624m	Hauenstein	
1,098m	Belchenflue	2 hours
492m	Balsthal	6 hours 30 mins

Stage 5: **Balsthal to Weissenstein** (20.5 kilometres)
492m	Balsthal	
1,230m	Höllchopfli	2 hours 45 mins
1,284m	Weissenstein	6 hours 15 mins

Stage 6: **Weissenstein to Frinvillier** (24 kilometres)
1,284m	Weissenstein	
1,444m	Hasenmatt	1 hour 40 mins
555m	Frinvillier	6 hours 30 mins

Stage 7: **Frinvillier to Chasseral** (18.5 kilometres)
555m	Frinvillier	
1,320m	Jurahaus (CAS hut)	3 hours 10 mins
1,548m	Chasseral	6 hours

Stage 8: **Chasseral to Neuchâtel** (21 kilometres)
1,548m	Chasseral	
1,087m	Chaumont	3 hours 20 mins
479m	Neuchâtel	5 hours

Stage 9: **Neuchâtel to Le Soliat** (23.5 kilometres)
479m	Neuchâtel	
1,235m	Fruitière de Bevaix	4 hours 50 mins
1,463m	Le Soliat	6 hours 30 mins

Stage 10:   **Le Soliat to Sainte-Croix**   (24 kilometres)
1,463m   Le Soliat
1,607m   Le Chasseron   5 hours
1,066m   Sainte-Croix   6 hours 30 mins

Stage 11:   **Sainte-Croix to Vallorbe**   (22.5 kilometres)
1,066m   Sainte-Croix
1,588m   Le Suchet   3 hours 10 mins
807m   Vallorbe   6 hours

Stage 12:   **Vallorbe to Col du Marchairuz**   (30.5 kilometres)
807m   Vallorbe
1,679m   Mont Tendre   6 hours 25 mins
1,447m   Col du Marchairuz   8 hours 30 mins

Stage 13:   **Col du Marchairuz to St. Cergue**   (16.5 kilometres)
1,447m   Col du Marchairuz
1,494m   Crêt de la Neuve   1 hour 20 mins
1,047m   St. Cergue   4 hours 30 mins

Stage 14:   **St. Cergue to Borex**   (18.5 kilometres)
1,047m   St. Cergue
1,677m   La Dôle   2 hours 20 mins
462m   Borex   5 hours 40 mins

*   *   *

PRINCIPAL ALTERNATIVE ROUTES OF THE JHR

The main Jura High Route follows the line of the eastern-most ridge of mountains almost throughout its length in Switzerland. However, since the Jura range consists of several parallel ridges, there are various options one could adopt on such a traverse, and the principal variants exploit some of these possibilities.

On Stage 4 the primary *Höhenweg* travels between Hauenstein and Balsthal, passing the splendid viewpoint of Belchenflue after two hours. At this point a Feeder route joins from Liestal (FR4). It is also the junction for the JHR Alternative which here initially runs more or less due west to Delémont and on to Les Rangiers where it links with the second Alternative JHR (A2) running from Basle (Dornach) to Geneva.

From Les Rangiers this major variant heads south-west along a ridge close to the French frontier to reach the classic vantage point of Vue des Alpes, then on to Noraigue before climbing to Le Soliat by the Creux du Van, thereby rejoining the main High Route at the end of Stage 9.

Options available to the long distance walker then, are summarised as follows:

a)   The main Jura High Route as described.
b)   The main JHR as described as far as Belchenflue, then break away on a westerly curve via Delémont, Les Rangiers and Vue des Alpes before returning to the main JHR at Le Soliat. (Outlined as A1 below.)
c)   The major JHR variant; Basle-Geneva, which runs from Dornach to Les Rangiers as A2 below, then follow A1 routes to Le Soliat.

Outline Alternative Stages
Alternative 1:
A1.1:   BELCHENFLUE-LANGENBRUCK-PASSWANG
BELCHENFLUE (1,098m) (2 hours from Hauenstein)
LANGENBRUCK (710m 1 hour 10 mins - Accommodation, supplies etc.)
CHELLENCHÖPFLI (1,157m 3 hours 30 mins)
OBER PASSWANG (1,094m 4 hours 45 mins - Naturfreundehaus, refreshments)

A1.2:   OBER PASSWANG-HOHE WINDE-DELEMONT
OBER PASSWANG (1,094m)
HOHE WINDE (1,204m 2 hours 15 mins)

Typical Jura pastureland seen from the ridge crest at Passwang - on the principal alternative A1.

OBER FRINGELI (826m 5 hours 55 mins - Accommodation, refreshments)
DELÉMONT (413m 9 hours 25 mins - Accommodation, supplies etc.)

A1.3: **DELÉMONT-LES RANGIERS (link with A2)**
DELÉMONT (413m)
LA HAUTE BORNE (888m 1 hour 50 mins - Accommodation, refreshments)
LES RANGIERS (865m 3 hours 25 mins - Accommodation, refreshments)

A1.4: **LES RANGIERS-ST.BRAIS-SAIGNELÉGIER**
LES RANGIERS (865m)
ST. BRAIS (967m 3 hours 20 mins - Accommodation, refreshments)
MONTFAUCON (996m 5 hours 10 mins - Accommodation, refreshments)
LE BÉMONT (982m 6 hours - Youth Hostel, refresh-

ments)
SAIGNELÉGIER (982m 6 hours 25 mins - Accommodation, supplies etc.)

A1.5: SAIGNELÉGIER-LA FERRIÈRE (link with FR7)-VUE DES ALPES
SAIGNELÉGIER (982m)
LE NOIRMONT (969m 1 hour 25 mins - Accommodation, supplies etc.)
LE BOÉCHET (1,033m 2 hours 50 mins - Accommodation, refreshments)
LA FERRIÉRE (1,005m 4 hours 40 mins - Refreshments)
VUE DES ALPES (1,283m 7 hours 25 mins - Accommodation, refreshments)

A1.6: VUE DES ALPES (link with FR8)-MONT RACINE-NORAIGUE-LE SOLIAT
VUE DES ALPES (1,283m)
TÊTE DE RAN (1,422m 50 mins - Accommodation, refreshments)
MONT RACINE (1,439m 2 hours)
LA TOURNE (1,129m 3 hours 10 mins - Refreshments)
NORAIGUE (728m 5 hours 45 mins - Accommodation, refreshments)
LE SOLIAT (1,463m 8 hours - Accommodation, refreshments)

Alternative 2: (Basle (Dornach)-Les Rangiers)
A2.1: DORNACH-BLAUENPASS-KLEINLÜTZEL
DORNACH (294m - Accommodation, refreshments, rail from Basle)
AESCH (312m 45 mins - Accommodation, refreshments)
BLAUENPASS (820m 3 hours)
KLEINLÜTZEL (421m Accommodation, supplies etc.)

A2.2: KLEINLÜTZEL-PLEIGNE-LES RANGIERS (link with A1.3)
KLEINLÜTZEL (421m)
MOVELIER (701m 2 hours 40 mins - Refreshments)
PLEIGNE (814m 3 hours 15 mins - Accommodation, refreshments)
LES CÔTES (905m 4 hours 45 mins)
LES RANGIERS (856m 5 hours 15 mins - Accommodation, refreshments)

FEEDER ROUTES

Several Feeder routes link the *Jura Höhenweg* with towns or villages situated away from the main ridges. Where these occur an indication is given in the descriptive text, and are summarised below.

FR1: **LAUFENBURG-OBERBOZBERG-BRUGG (link with JHR Stage 2)**
LAUFENBURG (318m Accommodation, refreshments)
SCHINBERG (722m 2 hours)
OBERBÖZBERG (539m 3 hours 50 mins - Accommodation refreshments)
BRUGG (352m 5 hours - Accommodation, supplies etc.)

FR1a: **LAUFENBERG-WIDACHER (link with JHR Stage 2)**
LAUFENBERG (318m Accommodation, refreshments)
SCHINBERG (722m 2 hours)
BINZACHER (Point 595) (595m 3 hours 40 mins)
WIDACHER (forest crosstracks) (572m 6 hours)

FR2: **FRICK-JUNKHOLZ-BÄNKERJOCH (link with JHR Stage 3)**
FRICK (360m Accommodation, refreshments)
GIPF-OBERFRICK (387m Accommodation, refreshments)
JUNKHOLZ (545m 1 hour 25 mins)
BÄNKERJOCH (668m 2 hours 45 mins)

FR3: **RHEINFELDEN-FARNSBURG-SCHAFMATT (2 Stages - link with JHR Stage 3)**
a) RHEINFELDEN (285m Accommodation, refreshments)
DORNHOF (462m 1 hour 20 mins - Refreshments)
HERSBERG (510m 2 hours 15 mins - Refreshments)
SISSACHER FLUE (699m 3 hours 30 mins - Refreshments)
FARNSBURG (642m 5 hours 20 mins - Refreshments, Postbus to Ormalingen (Accommodation)
b) ASPHOF (537m 6 hours 20 mins)
ANWIL (588m 8 hours 5 mins - Accommodation, refreshments)
SCHAFMATT (840m 9 hours 45 mins - Naturfreundehaus)

FR4: **LIESTAL-RAMLINSBURG-BELCHENFLUE (link with JHR Stage 4)**

LIESTAL (327m Accommodation, refreshments)
RAMLINSBURG (523m 1 hour 30 mins - Accommodation, refreshments)
ZUNZGERBERG (600m 2 hours)
OBER BELCHEN (890m 4 hours 45 mins - Accommodation, refreshments)
BELCHENFLUE (1,098m 5 hours 25 mins)

FR5: **LIESTAL-LUPSINGEN-PASSWANG (links with A1.1 & JHR 4 (via FR5b))**

a) LIESTAL (327m Accommodation, refreshments)
LUPSINGEN (439m 1 hour 25 mins - Refreshments)
EICH (685m 3 hours 25 mins)
PASSWANG (1,204m 5 hours 50 mins - junction of routes)

b) PASSWANG-LANGENBRUCK-BELCHENFLUE (link with JHR Stage 4)
PASSWANG (1,204m)
LANGENBRUCK (710m 3 hours - Accommodation, refreshments)
BELCHENFLUE (1,098m 4 hours 25 mins)

FR6: **DORNACH (Basle)-SEEWEN-PASSWANG (link with JHR 4 (via FR5b))**
DORNACH (294m - Accommodation, refreshments, rail from Basle)
SCHARTENFLUE (759m 1 hour 45 mins -Refreshments)
SEEWEN (544m 3 hours 20 mins - Accommodation, refreshments)
PASSWANG (1,204m 7 hours 25 mins - junction of routes)

FR7: **LA FERRIÈRE (A1.5)-RENAN-CHASSERAL (link with JHR Stage 7)**
LA FERRIÈRE (1,005m - Accommodation, refreshments)
LA PUCE (1,055m 1 hour - Accommodation, refreshments)
RENAN (889m 1 hour 10 mins - Refreshments)
CHASSERAL HOTEL (1,548m 5 hours - Accommodation, refreshments)

FR8: **CHASSERAL (JHR 7)-LE PÂQUIER-VUE VES ALPES (A1.6)**

CHASSERAL (1,548m - Accommodation, refreshments)
LE PÂQUIER (895m 1 hour 50 mins - Refreshments)
MONT d'AMIN (1,417m 4 hours 30 mins - CAS hut)
VUE DES ALPES (1,283m 5 hours 10 mins - Accommodation, refreshments)

* * *

USEFUL ADDRESSES

Map Suppliers:

McCarta Limited
122 Kings Cross Road
London WC1X 9DS

Edward Stanford Ltd
12-14 Long Acre
London WC2

The Map Shop
15 High Street
Upton-upon-Severn
Worcs. WR8 0HJ

Rand McNally Map Store
10 East 53rd Street
New York
N.Y.

Also available from the Swiss National Tourist Office.

Tourist Information Offices:
Many towns and villages along the route of the JHR have their own Tourist Information Offices, but in addition the following addresses may be useful for advance planning.
Swiss National Tourist Office
Swiss Centre
New Coventry Street
London. W1V 8EE

Nordwestschweizerische Verkehrsvereinigung
Blumenrain 2
CH 4001 Basel
(For the cantons of Aargau, Basel-land, Basel-Stadt and Solothurn)

Office Jurassien du Tourisme
12 Place de la Gare
Case postale
CH 2800 Delémont
(For the canton Jura)

Office du Tourisme du Jura bernois
26 Avenue de la Poste
CH 2740 Moutier
(For the Bernese Jura)

Office Neuchâtelois du Tourisme
9 Rue de Tresor
(Place des Halles)
Case postale 1418
CH 2000 Neuchâtel
(For canton Neuchâtel)

Office du Tourisme du Canton de Vaud
3 Avenue de Mon-Repos
CH 1005 Lausanne
(For the cantons of Geneva and Vaud)

Swiss National Tourist Offices in North America

104 South Michigan Avenue
Chicago
Il 60603

608 Fifth Avenue
New York
NY 10020

250 Stockton Street
San Francisco
CA 94108

P.O. Box 215
Commerce Court West
Toronto
Ontario
M5L 1E8

Youth Hostels Associations:

Schweizerischer Bund für Jugendherbergen
St. Alban-Rheinweg 170
Postfach 3229
CH 3001 Berne 22

YHA (England & Wales)
Trevelyan House
8 St. Stephen's Hill
St. Albans, Herts. AL1 2DY
(Membership of YHA is valid in hostels worldwide).

*   *   *

THE JURA

Winter Ski Traverses
R. Brian Evans

Photos by the Author

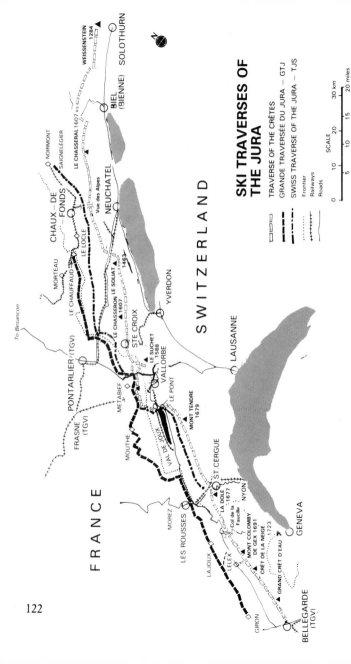

SKI TRAVERSES OF THE JURA

TRAVERSE OF THE CRÊTES
GRANDE TRAVERSÉE DU JURA – GTJ
SWISS TRAVERSE OF THE JURA – TJS
Frontier
Railways
Roads

SCALE

0   5   10   15   20   30 km
          0   10   15   20 miles

FRANCE

SWITZERLAND

To Besançon

SOLOTHURN
WEISSENSTEIN 1284
BIEL (BIENNE)
NOIRMONT
SAIGNELÉGIER
LE CHASSERAL 1607
CHAUX–DE–FONDS
NEUCHATEL
Vue des Alpes
MORTEAU
LE LOCLE
1463
LE CHAUFFAUD
LE CHASSERON LE SOLIAT
1607
STE CROIX
YVERDON
PONTARLIER ('TGV')
LE SUCHET 1588
VALLORBE
FRASNE (TGV)
METABIEF
LE PONT
MONT TENDRE 1679
LAUSANNE
MOUTHE
VAL DE JOUX
ST. CERGUE
LA DOLE 1677
NYON
MOREZ
Col de la Faucille
LES ROUSSES
MONT COLOMBY DE GEX 1691
CRÊT DE LA NEIGE 1723
GENEVA
LAJOUX
LÉLEX
GRAND CRÊT D'EAU
GIRON
BELLEGARDE (TGV)

122

CONTENTS

Introduction 125
Dangers 126
By Car to the Jura in Winter 126
Ski de Fond in the Jura 127
Equipment 128
Maps 128
Winter in the Jura 129
Snow Conditions 130
Piste Skiing 131
Skiing Off-piste 134
Where to Stay 136
The Traverses of the Jura 138

The GTJ: Grande Traversée du Jura .141
   Le Chauffaud to Les Hôpitaux Neufs 143
   Les Hôpitaux Neufs to La Cure (Les Rousses) 148
   La Cure (Les Rousses) to Giron 153

The Traverse of the Swiss Jura (TJS) 157

Traverse of the Crêtes 160
   Weissenstein to Vue des Alpes 161
   Vue des Alpes to Jougne 163
   Jougne to La Givrine 167
   La Givrine to Menthières 171

Circuit of the Val de Joux 176

Useful Addresses 182
Route Maps 184

*A typical Jura scene - fresh snow in the
early morning sunshine!*

INTRODUCTION

The purpose of this section of the book is twofold. First to point out the vast possibilities for enjoyable winter walking on skis in the Jura; and second to encourage those walkers and backpackers who have not yet taken to skis that they are missing an unforgettable experience. Certainly cross-country skiing changed my approach to winter and although devotees of Scotland claim that the skiing is wonderful there, my advice is to head for continental Europe. You may get bad weather but the chances of good weather and good snow conditions are so much better than in Britain that there can be no comparison. Even when the weather is bad you rarely get the accompanying gales so prevalent in Britain. On a poor day you can still enjoy sheltered skiing in the forests.

There is so much skiing in the Jura that this guide can only touch the surface. The French call it the *grandes espaces* and truly when covered in deep snow you travel long distances without taking skis off. There are few walls, fences are buried, the occasional road is crossed with care, but generally you travel long unbroken mountain sides, combes and forests.

In this guide I have attempted to give enough information to set you in the right direction and to assess whether you think you will enjoy the nature of the skiing. Much is left to individual initiative. There is no point in giving day-by-day descriptions as times, and even routes, will vary enormously with conditions and your preferred approach of lightweight *gîte d'etape* or the heavier loads of spartan backpacking.

Unladen experts can travel the pistes at incredible speeds. You may be lucky enough to see racers, who will be travelling in a few hours the distance you may cover in a week. Novices must plan short days and take care not to overestimate their capabilities. Even the pistes can be slow after a snowfall, for the piste machines have their priorities on the shorter circuits around their village base.

The Jura is ideal country to travel through and the rewards of a journey passing a variety of scenery is more rewarding than short circuits from a single base - although most of the skiers you meet are holidaymakers or weekenders based on a centre. Greater satisfaction comes from the accomplishment of a planned route with a fresh scene every day and a new lodging every night.

Dangers

The Jura is one of the safest areas in Europe for cross-country skiing. The terrain is usually easy, civilization never far away. The machine pisted trails present no danger for it takes a great depth of new snow to hide all trace of the track. The main ski trails are well signed and you will usually meet other skiers. Novices should stick to the marked routes until experience is gained.

Off the piste new snow quickly hides all ski tracks, so you cannot rely on returning in your tracks in bad visibility. Even summer roads may be eradicated and it takes a practised eye to pick out and follow the line of a snow buried path through the forest. Despite the absence of sharp mountain terrain the long open combes and dense forests of the Jura pose their own navigational problems in bad visibility, especially to the skier on a day outing. The backpacker will have his warm sleeping bag, stove and possibility of shelter in one of the many huts or farms. The day skier needs to make certain there is enough daylight to return to base.

Beginners must allow themselves plenty of time to complete an outing as time can be swallowed by falls or waiting for the party to congregate. Avalanche danger in the Jura is negligible, although there are places where skilful judgement and experience is called for, particularly on the higher crest.

By Car to the Jura in Winter

Winter driving to European ski resorts is becoming much more popular amongst British ski enthusiasts and with several people sharing, the cost can be very economical. Your departure ferry will vary according to location; most living in the south will travel Dover-Calais and join the French autoroute system to Dijon for the central Jura; to Nantua for the southern Jura; or Besancon for northern Jura. For those living north of the Midlands an alternative is to travel from Felixstowe or Hull to the Belgian ports. A night's sleep on the crossing will enable you to reach the Jura the following day. For northern Jura go via Brussels, Luxembourg, Strasbourg, Belfort; for central Jura to Luxembourg, Nancy, Besancon; for southern Jura to Nancy, Toul, Dijon, Dole. This has the advantage of cheap fuel in Luxembourg, at least until 1992.

Note that if you go into Switzerland you will be required to pay an autoroute tax of 30SF, valid for a year. If you intend to use only minor roads in the Swiss Jura you should be allowed in without paying this tax, but in other parts it is very easy to stray onto a section of motorway and the fine is heavy.

Motorway tolls in France are high. From Calais you will be on toll-roads most of the way; via Brussels the only toll-road is from Toul to Dijon.

Conditions of winter driving through France and Belgium should be no different to England. Strong winds diminish as you near the Jura. Once in the hills, the main roads are quickly cleared of snow but minor roads are likely to have a snow covering and chains may be required. On the steeper minor roads chains are compulsory when conditions require them. Local supermarkets and garages sell snow chains at about half the price available in Britain.

A car gives greater flexibility and convenience and it is still possible to complete a traverse and return by train to your starting point by using the frequent train and bus service which operates on the Swiss side of the Jura.

Ski de Fond in the Jura

In France over 2 million people participate in ski de fond, on 10,000km of prepared pistes at 410 cross-country ski stations. Every year sees more enthusiasts taking to the sport, as downhill, or alpine skiing becomes more and more expensive.

Until recently the communes bore the cost of preparing the pistes, - not only the actual winter costs of machinery and manpower, but the autumn cost of preparing trails: cutting branches, moving rocks, placing signs etc. In 1986 a voluntary ticket could be bought to offset some of the cost. In 1987 this was made compulsory, as not enough income was generated voluntarily. As one Frenchman commented 'The French are not Swiss'. In Switzerland skiers are asked to pay a voluntary seasonal contribution of 30SF.

To use the pistes in France, skiers must buy either a day, week or season tickets. In 1988 a season ticket at 100FF, just over £10, was valid throughout France, excellent value when compared with the cost of a day downhill skiing. A week ticket was 75FF.

In the Jura the ticket is valid for trails in France or Switzerland, which makes the French ticket a better bargain than the Swiss. You may say that you are going to ski off-piste, but in practice it is difficult to avoid prepared pistes at some stage of the trip, and in all likelihood you will be glad to use them.

The term *ski de fond* really refers to the equivalent of jogging. Its exponents can be seen in lightweight skin-tight track suits, racing round the pistes. Readers of this book will probably be more interested in using skis as a means to see the countryside - *randonnée nordique* - which is normally a day's tour not always on the piste. *Raid nordique* is the term for a backpacking trip of several days, usually more off the piste than on. This requires experience and equipment for mountain walking in winter conditions.

Equipment

Skis, sticks and boots can be hired at all the major centres, at the various *foyers de ski de fond*, or ski hire shops. Alternatively you could buy the equipment in Britain or abroad. The cheapest package is adequate, but take care to choose reasonably warm, watertight boots. Some of the cheaper boots do not last long before they leak. There is no need to buy skis with metal edges, unless you intend to use them on the icy fells of Britain.

Choose touring skis rather than the extremely narrow racing skis, especially if you intend going off-piste where broader skis do not sink in quite so far. Length can be measured from floor to arm-extended wrist. Sticks should be about armpit height. Novices should buy no wax-skis. These are skis with a patterned base which affords grip for walking uphill. When you have had your money's worth of a cheap package, you will then have the experience to choose whether to buy more sophisticated skis. Experts swear that waxed skis go far better than the no-wax variety, but I am sure you will feel that you are going quite fast enough without!

It is worth taking some silver wax. Sometimes you find the snow sticks to the base of the ski and application of silver wax will help alleviate the problem. Sunglasses are preferable to goggles - which tend to steam up especially when going uphill. An increasingly popular alternative is a sun visor, a boon to wearers of spectacles. Some suncream and lip salve is essential.

Clothing is really a matter of commonsense. Winter walkers will know what to expect and their usual clothing is recommended. You can get hot with the exertion, but you need warm clothing, wind and waterproof. Gaiters keep snow out of the ski-boots.

If you are backpacking be prepared for a big drop in temperature once the sun has set. The area around the central Jura is renowned for being the coldest place in France or Switzerland. Mouthe is known as Little Siberia and temperatures down to -20°C are common.

Maps

The Jura is a big area and to cover the entire region with the best maps would require a considerably outlay. For the southern and central areas the best general maps are the 1:50,000 Didier & Richard No.33 Au Coeur du Jura and No.34 Jura Sud. These maps, although rather fussy, show ski routes in red, and various refuges, shelters and ski de fond foyers. Note that the routes are suggestions - and do not always coincide with pisted trails or even signed paths. The refuges marked are not always reliable. However, the maps cover a vast area and are excellent value for money.

There is a map series specifically designed for the skier - 1:25,000 Ski de Fond, Massif du Jura, Nos.1 to 6. Each map costs about £5 and covers a relatively small area. Designed mainly to show the GTJ and its neighbouring trails, the maps are excellent. They show the pistes, the refuges and *gîtes d'etape*, but background detail is sometimes difficult to decipher. If you intend staying around one area, these are the maps to buy. Maps 2 to 6 are sufficient for the GTJ, as map one shows a northern feeder. The maps are on sale locally.

Cartes Nationales de la Suisse are available in both 1:50,000 and 1:25,000. The 1:25,000 are beautiful maps and are recommended for off-piste touring as they show the terrain with admirable clarity. They do not mark ski trails or refuges and it is wise to obtain the tourist leaflets of the areas to be visited. You can then attempt to tie up the tourist information with the map. Especially useful for the excellent Val de Joux are maps 1221 Le Sentier, 1241 Marchairuz, and 1201 Mouthe. The latter includes the Mont d'Or area. Useful maps for the Swiss traverses are the Kümmerly & Frey Wanderkarte des Jura 1:50,000 Sheets 3,4,5 and 6.

Winter in the Jura

Snow transforms the Jura into a wonderland of great beauty. The forests are breathtaking when the trees are clothed in a heavy white mantle, especially when sunshine adds a jewel-like sparkle to the scene. Even on days of mist, a trip into the forest is very rewarding, with intimate views of ice-caked trees, animal tracks going seemingly irrationally in all directions, birds trying to pick the seeds from the exposed pines or any remaining berries. On a clear day leave the forests behind and mount steadily to the highest crests where the view is absolutely stunning. Below, barely visible under a light cloak of mist, lies Lake Geneva; across the Swiss plain are the Alps, displayed in a tremendous wall. It is an interesting exercise to identify as many peaks as you can, from the obvious - Mont Blanc, standing like a giant blancmange head and shoulders above the rest, the tooth of the Dru, the dark wedge of the Grandes Jorasses, the crenellated crest of the Dents du Midi, the dark triangle of the Eiger - to the old friends of the connoisseur: the ice-covered slabs of the Bargy, the proud point of Percée, and so on ... Best of all, on a short winter day, is to linger on

Intimate forest views weave a pattern of light and shade.

the crest near sunset, when the Alps are lit with a magical rosy glow -
then swoop down to your nights lodging and a warm fire.

I think that winter is the most beautiful season to visit the Jura and
the only way to explore the area in snow is to travel on skis. If you
can't ski, don't worry. On many of my winter trips we have included
novices in the party, and their progress has been remarkable. Remember at least 50% of the trip is uphill and much of the downhill is very
gentle. It doesn't take more than a couple of hours to be able to cope
with that sort of skiing. As the holiday progresses, more confidence is
gained until you are rattling down the tracks with gay abandon.

Snow Conditions
The season lasts from December to Easter, with most snow coverage
usually in January and February. The first snow of any quantity
comes to the Jura in December, but cannot be relied on. Christmas is
uncertain - 1983/4/5 were virtually snowless; in 1986 there was so
much snow as to be almost overwhelming. Christmas 1987 was again
snowless and by the end of January the resorts were getting really
worried. However, by the end of February there was a superabund-
ance of deep snow which lasted late into the season.

130

Once a deep snowfall has occurred, it settles, is topped up regularly and provides magnificent touring. A fall of deep powder snow stays powdery if the temperatures are low - and makes progress off the piste very fatiguing. If temperatures rise after a heavy snow fall, even if it rains, the snow consolidates and can provide good off-piste running, especially at higher levels. A thaw, then a freeze, can result in that most abominable of off-piste snow; breakable crust. Best touring snow of all is found in the longer days of March and April when the sun softens the top few inches, yet the base remains firm. Off-piste on the highest crests is fabulous in those conditions.

Piste Skiing

Most first time ski tourers will prefer to use the pistes and the above remarks on snow conditions do not apply, unless you are unfortunate enough to catch a section which has not been machined after a heavy snowfall! Once a piste has been groomed by the purpose-built machines, it provides good skiing. The machines tend to look after the shorter circuits close to base first. After a period of hard trail breaking in deep powder, the piste comes as a welcome relief and many scornful off-piste skiers have to swallow their pride and admit that 'motorway' skiing has its good points.

Piste machines lay grooved ski tracks

Every little ski village has its ski de fond circuits which are well marked. At the larger resorts, maps of the pistes are available at the Syndicat d'Initiative or the ski de fond foyers. Usually at the start of the pistes is a board which shows all the circuits, their colour codes and lengths. Always they are coded according to length - green less than 5km, blue 5-10km, red 10-18km, black more than 18km. Sometimes there are chevrons which denote difficulty. One arrow denotes little difficulty, two arrows medium difficulty and three arrows quite difficult. Icy conditions can increase the grade. In practice, the black are usually little different from the blue except in length, so a ski tour can incorporate any track. Most of the pistes follow forest roads, which provide reasonably gentle gradients and are wide enough for the machine to pass. Newcomers should find little difficulty in negotiating such pistes, especially uphill. The lightweight, narrow, cross-country touring skis are remarkably easy to manage on a straightforward track.

The caterpillar tracked machines create a ploughed 'lane' between 10ft. and 20ft. wide with two pairs of precision grooves for skis. On popular tracks there are often three lanes, one of which is left smooth for exponents of the more rapid, graceful skating technique. There are rules of the road - you should keep in the right-hand track, groups should travel single file not abreast and if you stop, step out of the tracks and onto the edge. It is sometimes disconcerting when faster skiers swoop past, but presumably the faster skier is good enough to wend around slow parties.

Undulating tracks are easy to cope with; you just stand in the tracks and go. Steeper slopes are more unnerving as speed is gained - it might feel like the TGV, but it is never as fast as it seems and a fall is more a matter of a laugh and hurt pride than a serious calamity. Downhill bends are more difficult for the novice - you tend to shoot out of the tracks onto the soft edge which with its immediate slowing effect causes a head first dive into the snow.

Having fallen down, the problem is getting up. On the hard piste there is little difficulty. In deep snow it can be exhausting. Cross your ski sticks to make a firm base to press upon, having already swung your legs downhill and parallel to the slope. In very deep soft powder, especially when carrying a heavy sack, you may need to unfasten the skis first, or even accept assistance.

There are various methods of descent and all have their uses. The most basic is to summon up your courage and go, gathering speed until you either reach easier angled terrain or decide that it is safer to 'bomb out' with a 'sit stop'. A more cautious descent can be made by using the sticks as a brake. You can hold both sticks in one hand and

The machine-groomed piste provides easy skiing.

press the spikes firmly into the snow, rather like an ice axe glissading brake. Or, more elegantly, hold the sticks halfway down and lodge the top of the pole in front of the shoulders. Even a steep slope with bends can be safely descended by the novice skier in this fashion. The only danger is of forming bad habits and lapsing into this form of descent every time rather than polish up genuine technique. Another useful technique for descending is to keep one ski in the tracks and use the other out of the track in a snow-plough position. This requires some skill and practice, as does the full snow-plough. A useful means of slowing is to press both skis outwards into the outer edge of the grooved track.

Cross-country ski manuals tend to confuse the beginner with a multitude of techniques, many of which are only of use to those interested in ski running. Anyone who intends to use cross-country skis purely as a means of winter walking or backpacking can get away with a minimum of technique, which in no way impairs enjoyment. My advice is that if you are a keen walker or backpacker, then a pair of cross-country skis will open up a whole new world of winter enjoyment.

If you have tried cross-country skiing in Britain don't be disillusioned. My experience of British conditions is one of utter frustration. There is usually too little snow, an abundance of rock poking through, hazardous icy patches or hard windblown snow - like trying to ski on a switchback of corrugations. Utterly heartbreaking for the novice and totally unlike the conditions abroad. In the Jura there is plenty of snow, with plenty of room to try techniques and no harm if you fall.

Many downhill alpine ski resorts have tried to break into the cross-country market by creating *loipes* or pisted circuits. You may have seen these and dismissed cross-country as being merely going for a run on skis around a field. It couldn't be further from the truth! Most alpine resorts are too steep for good cross-country - the best terrain is undulating plateaux and that is exactly what you get in the Jura, with mile upon mile of undulating country, forest and clearing, bare open summits and long upland combes which offer tremendous scope for day walks or expeditions or *raids* of several days.

Skiing off-piste
Off-piste touring is the most rewarding for experienced skiers. For keen mountain walkers this is the type of skiing to aim for, perhaps after an apprenticeship skiing the pistes.

It requires all the skills of safe mountain travel, familiarity with compass and map reading. In a prolonged spell of good weather there will be trails radiating everywhere, for the Jura is a popular area. In bad weather trails are obliterated within a few hours.

The forest trails can be confusing especially if there are no tracks to follow. It is wise to obtain a ski piste leaflet from the local tourist office and keep track of where you are before branching off into untracked forest. It is so easy to blindly follow other peoples' trails. If you keep a constant check on your whereabouts you will be able to branch off with confidence. Sometimes even forest roads can be so covered with snow that it is difficult to see their whereabouts. Summer paths are almost impossible to identify. Look for the wooden signs on trees, sometimes so encrusted with snow that they are easy to miss. In light forest it is not always easy to see where the route lies. Often it does not matter, so long as you are heading in your general direction and the forest does not become too dense.

Always try to keep a mental map of the area and your position. After a heavy snow fall all the ski tracks are obliterated - so do not rely on

134

After heavy snowfall, trail-breaking can be arduous.

following other peoples' trails, or returning from a high hut on your own tracks.

On open slopes skiing in bad visibility is a wierd experience akin to floating in a white cloud. You cannot sense speed or gradient in a white out. The same difficulties are encountered towards evening when the light is fading. In these conditions I have skied over a cornice which was completely invisible; fortunately the drop was only 15ft. into deep soft snow, but it shows the need for care. Hopefully you will be skiing in good conditions when making your own route in perfect snow is a rewarding experience.

The most fatiguing part of an off-piste trip is trail breaking. In good conditions you will sink an inch or two, after several days of continual heavy snowfall progress becomes so arduous that you would be best advised to head for the nearest piste system or road. In between, trail breaking is manageable but should be shared by the strongest members of the party.

Where to Stay
Accommodation in the Jura is plentiful. There are numerous towns and villages close to the ski areas, plenty of hotels, apartments, gîtes and huts. The area is very popular and in peak holiday periods much of the accommodation is fully booked.

School holidays are best avoided but they spread over a broad period. They have Christmas-New Year, Easter and a winter half-term. France is split into two zones for school holidays which creates an extended peak period from mid February to early March and mid April to early May.

Accommodation lists can be obtained from the various Syndicat's d'Initiative or Comité Départemental du Tourisme (see addresses p.182).

If you choose to use the cheaper accommodation which is available, then a few comments may be useful. In the mountain areas many of the hotels will have various grades of accommodation, including the cheapest - dortoirs. These are dormitories with bunks, similar to hostels but with no segregation of the sexes. Similar dormitory accommodation is available at several of the Foyers de Ski de Fond and at many Gîtes d'Étape. They have central heating, hot showers and meals can usually be bought if required. Some of the gîtes have self-cooking facilities, others may allow you to cook on your own stoves.

Along the GTJ there is a chain of gîtes, but the route is so popular that you may have difficulty if you do not book in advance. There is a scheme whereby you can send a single booking to Étapes Jura, who will book you into six consecutive refuges along the GTJ south, or the GTJ north or a circuit of the southern section. Daily stages are between 20 and 25 kilometres. (See addresses p.182.)

The committed mountain backpacker may prefer to use the unguarded huts and refuges which exist in the Jura. There are several foresters' huts owned by the communes. These are either stone chalets or timber refuges. These are not for the squeamish, for some could be described as squalid. The advantages of using this type of accommodation - apart from the cost, which is negligible - are many. You get a true feel of wilderness in a primitive shelter deep in the forest especially if you have to dig your way in through deep snow. Wood has to be gathered, the stove lit and nursed through its initial smoky period. Needless to say, if you stay at these simple shelters you need full winter backpacking equipment - good sleeping bag, sleeping mat, stove, cooking equipment, and all your food. Drinking water is obtained by melting snow - take care to scoop up uncontaminated snow! If there have been no falls of snow for several days, coffee filter paper or a handkerchief is handy, to filter out pine needles, twigs and other extraneous matter. A plastic carrier bag is useful for storing snow, since one panful melts to a mere eyeful.

The wood burning stoves can be of conventional type, or more like an oven with a small fire box. Both types need careful handling, but throw out a lot of heat once they are going. Usually there is a good deal of eye-smarting woodsmoke until the flue gets hot. It pays to take a little firelighter and dry paper. If you are lucky there will be a supply of kindling and logs at the hut, and a saw. Sometimes we have found razor-sharp foresters' axes. You are asked to replace whatever you use and leave the huts in a clean and tidy condition. Dead wood is plentiful in the forest. Particularly useful are the lower dead branches of the large pine trees.

Sometimes these huts have a wooden floored sleeping area upstairs, occasionally with mattresses. Sometimes they are so small that you have to squeeze in any way you can, sleeping on the floor and even the table. Toilet facilities are good - you just ski off into the forest and find a private niche behind a suitable tree.

The French and Swiss rarely use these huts, seemingly preferring comfort to character. In several visits we have only once encountered another party heading for a simple refuge, perhaps as well, for in many cases our party only just squeezed in. Perhaps the most original refuge is a converted tramcar on the slopes of Mont Tendre. A night there is an unforgettable experience. There are several refuges of the Swiss and French Alpine Clubs, which compared to the foresters' huts, are positively luxurious. It is not wise to rely on these huts however, for they are often open only at weekends, unless a party has booked them and obtained the key.

In Switzerland some refuges marked on maps and some of the foresters' cabins have signs prohibiting an overnight stay except in emergency. However, we have been directed to one excellent hut of this type by a border gendarme patrolman and in practice it seems that a night stay in winter is tolerated.

Even more spartan accommodation is available to those who take a tent. I prefer to carry a lightweight dome tent, which takes the place of exposure bags for two people. With it comes freedom of mind, for you do not have the hassle of getting to the next gîte, or telephoning ahead to find somewhere not booked up. It is hardly practical to pitch in soft deep snow but many of the high farms leave a cowshed or basement open where you can enjoy the most unusual of sleeping quarters. A tent pitched inside an empty, draughty cowshed soon warms up with the stove going, and can be surprisingly comfortable for the well equipped.

The Traverses of the Jura

There are three main ski traverses and many permutations. The most popular traverse is the French GTJ, the Grande Traversée du Jura. This follows in the main, the secondary crest with excursions into the combes on either side. The GTJ is the French winter equivalent of the Pennine Way and is so popular that you will surely not travel alone.

The Swiss TJS starts a little further north-east than the GTJ and follows a crest parallel to the GTJ, which it joins for the crossing of the busy valley around Metabief. From the flanks of Mont d'Or the TJS branches south across delightful country to Le Pont, the gateway to the beautiful Val de Joux. From here the route follows a high combe just below the crest of Mont Tendre to end at La Givrine. The TJS is not nearly so well pisted or popular as the GTJ and is a highly recommended mix of trails.

The third traverse is the Traverse of the Crêtes - the integral traverse of the highest ridge, following more or less the line of the summer High Route described in this book. In practice the true crest is often too windblown or icy so a more comfortable ski route is sought on the shelves which lie just a little way down the north-west slopes, and hold snow well into the season. The winter route begins at Weissenstein, follows a narrowish crest past Le Chasseron, takes the variant past Vue des Alpes and descends into the Gorges of the Areuse at Noraigue. From the Creux du Van the broad plateau is traversed to

Ste. Croix, with the option of taking the summit of Le Chasseral on the way. Thence over Le Suchet to Jougne, across Mont d'Or, the long switchback of Mont Tendre, or the easier pistes of the TJS. The final section, in France, is the most mountainous of the Jura and in good conditions the most rewarding - from Le Dôle, over the Colomby de Gex and the Crêt de la Neige to finish across a sharp arête, before descending to Menthières. The persistent can tick off the last summit, the Crêt d'Eau on the way.

This traverse is not for inexperienced skiers. It is a long mountain route (2 weeks or more) which will test the ability of the seasoned ski mountaineer. It requires good snow conditions as most of it is on unpisted snow. In the clear air of winter, the views of the Alps are tremendous.

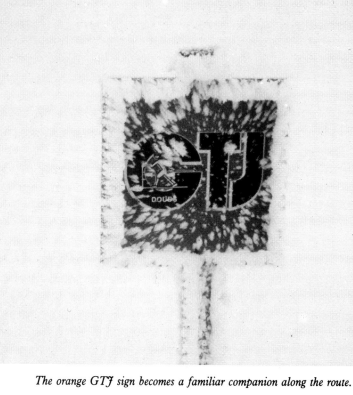

The orange GTJ sign becomes a familiar companion along the route.

THE GTJ
GRANDE TRAVERSÉE
DU JURA

170km   8/10 days

The French GTJ was established to cater for the enormous number of people who want the challenge of a long distance route on skis. Much of it lies on or close to the summer GR5 and it is the winter equivalent of a long distance footpath which traverses the three *Departements* of the Jura - Doubs, Jura and Ain. The trail lies mainly in France, with one incursion into Switzerland.

The route hovers around the 1,000m level, rising to 1,300m in places. The trail is generally well groomed by piste machines, and the skiing is always easy. In reasonable conditions there are few problems as the trail is well signed. Originally designed for travelling north to south, it can be traversed equally well the other way, although steeper descents are encountered in places.

The GTJ is around 170km and takes about eight to ten days. There are five links into the principal route and an extension across the Bugey. The Swiss TJS runs parallel for a considerable distance and offers scope for an interesting circuit.

The standard of skiing is very easy, as it lies almost entirely on prepared pistes, often using forest roads. If you like to bomb along and cover distance in pleasant scenery, this would suit you. If you prefer more adventurous surroundings and the challenge of route finding, you may be bored at times. Its charm is gentle rather than spectacular, forest rather than mountain. You may go for long periods without distant views, but the intimate scenery of snow-decked pines is quite charming. When views do open out they reveal long forested crests separated by broad white combes. Distant views of the Alps are lacking from the GTJ, blocked by the neighbouring higher parallel crest. If the day is clear, a diversion to the summit of Mont d'Or is highly recommended as this will reveal the Alps.

You will certainly enjoy the cameraderie which evolves on a long distance route, as you meet up with the same groups of skiers on the way. Some of the groups are guided, accompanied by *moniteurs*, and

141

have their equipment ferried by vehicle. This is the easiest way to do the route, although you have to pay for the privilege. There are many organisations which offer tours along the GTJ, see the list at the end of the book p.182.

You will need to be adequately fit, and novices may find the distance between some stages stretching. In a period of bad weather the route becomes more serious for the trail may be obliterated until the piste machines arrive. Some sections, particularly between Les Cernets and Les Fourgs may not be machine pisted and will need heavy trail breaking. In this case the best advice is to linger at the gîte and let other more experienced or enthusiastic skiers bear the brunt.

Several villages are passed where provisions can be bought. Most French parties travel very light, eat at restaurants en route and stay at gîtes d'étape which are spread along the route. The gîtes d'étape vary considerably from tiny converted sections of farmhouses to sophistic-ated ferme auberges which provide meals of excellent quality. The cost in 1988 was between 30 and 40FF overnight, or 120-130FF for evening meal, bed and breakfast. Some of these gîtes are quite small and quickly get booked up. It is almost essential to book in advance, or phone the next gîte along the way, especially if your party consists of more than two persons. The staff at the gîtes are very helpful and will often ring ahead for you if you have difficulty with the language. You can reserve gîtes in advance by writing to Étapes Jura, Bureau des gîtes Lajoux, 39310 Septmoncel, France.

Backpacking gear increases the load but as the ascents are not ferocious, some may prefer the freedom which comes with this mode of travel. It enables the party to use several unguarded refuges along the way, and although my parties have rarely encountered others, there is always the possibility that they may be full. There are so many tiny villages close to the route, that some form of accommodation could always be found.

The start of the GTJ at Chauffaud can be reached by train to Morteau. Nearest TGV station is at Pontarlier. The usual end of the route at Giron is not far from Bellegarde (TGV). Car based travellers are advised to leave the vehicle at Chauffaud and return by train from Bellegarde, via Geneva, Neuchâtel and Le Locle. The Swiss railways provide an excellent service. Shortened versions of the route can also be planned, with a return to base by train from Ste. Croix, Vallorbe, or La Cure.

Addresses and phone numbers of key gîtes are noted in the text.

Abbreviations: M = meals provided   S/C = self cooking facilities provided.

Sometimes gîtes without self cooking facilities will allow you to prepare your own meal on your own equipment.

GTJ
LE CHAUFFAUD to LES HÔPITAUX NEUFS
53km   3 days

Maps: Ski de Fond Massif du Jura Sheets 2 and 3 1:25,000 or
Kümmerly & Frey Wanderkarte des Jura Sheet 5 1:50,000
(This shows most of the route but does not mark ski trails.
Useful if you are doing a circuit.)
Didier & Richard Sheets 32 and 33 - a lot of map for a little
corner!

	KM.	ACC.KM.	
Le Chauffaud	0.00	0.00	Gîte
Pièrre a Feu	3.50	3.50	
Le Gardot	4.00	7.50	
Vieux Chateleu	5.00	12.50	Gîte
Les Seignes	4.25	16.75	Gîte 1km
Grands Cernets	10.00	26.75	Gîte
Verrières de Joux	5.00	31.75	Gîte 1km
Auberge de Tillau	5.50	37.25	Gîte
Granges Bailly	5.00	42.25	Gîte
Les Fourgs	2.50	44.75	Gîte
Les Hôpitaux Neufs	8.25	53.00	Gîte 2km

This first section of the GTJ starts along a slim crest, which has plenty of road access points and popular ski de fond circuits. After Les Seignes a much quieter stretch passes through Switzerland to Les Cernets, after which a steep descent is made to a busy main road and rail valley at Verrières de Joux. The crossing of the upland between here and Les Fourgs is quite delightful, to join the very popular ski pistes which lead to Les Hôpitaux, one of several villages in a major road passage through the Jura. There is plenty of accommodation here, and opportunities to link into other routes for a return through Switzerland. Shopping possibilities are few until Les Fourgs is reached.

CAF Gîte Les Tavaillons, Le Chauffaud - the start of the GTJ.

The GTJ commences at **Le Chauffaud**, a small hamlet at 1,072m above the *cluse*[1] of La Ranconnière. The spectacular Col des Roches, which marks the frontier, is pierced by a road tunnel. On the Swiss side lies the busy town of Le Locle; on the French side, in the Ain valley is Villars-le-Lac. A narrow lane branches off at Col France to Le Chauffaud. Chains may be required. There is plenty of parking space at Le Chauffaud, although it is best to ask at the gîte for advice. Access by train is via Frasne (TGV) and Pontarlier (TGV), then local train to Morteau where taxis are available for the final 12km. If you are returning to Le Chauffaud through Switzerland there is an almost hourly train service from Neuchâtel to Le Locle, but taxis do not cross the frontier and you will have to walk the final 8km.

CAF Gîte Les Tavaillons, Le Chauffaud, 25130 Villars-le-Lac,
Tel: 81.68.12.55. (M. S/C).
The ideal starting point, a comfortable, friendly gîte. *Tavaillons* are the thin squares of bark used so often in the Jura for weatherproofing the sides of buildings. The gîte is popular and invariably booked up on

1. A *Cluse* is a steep sided craggy right-angled break through the long crest. They are a prominent natural feature of the Jura and provide a convenient passage for roads, railways and occasionally rivers.

144

Friday and Saturday nights. An alternative smaller gîte is La Petite Ferme, 25130 Villars-le-Lac. Tel: 81.68.02.81 or 81.68.08.33. (S/C), or Sur la Roche, Le Chauffaud. Tel: 81.68.08.94.

The ski trail starts in a combe just by Le Chauffaud and more or less follows the line of the road to reach the Fromagerie de Chauffaud, where the first orange sign - GTJ km1 - lies just below the road. These will become familiar and generally the route is so well signed that route finding is easy; however, there are a few places where confusion may arise, particularly where pistes radiate or have been obliterated by fresh snow. Orange is reserved for the GTJ, other trails are marked with either blue, green or red, but beware of dayglow orange markers which are sometimes used as substitutes on red trails!

The trail undulates gently to **Pièrre a Feu** (Ferme auberge, restaurant, ski centre). Call at the Ski Centre to buy your GTJ pass, which is obligatory. Maps can be bought here and they will telephone ahead to book the next gîte. Pièrre a Feu is a busy little downhill ski area.

Leave the buzzing swarm of skiers to cross a clearing into the forest past la Saule, a large open chalet on the right, then almost level to **Le Gardot**.

We arrived to find crowds of people lining the trail, loudspeakers blaring, drinks at the ready - not for us, but for the race leaders who were just arriving in a long snake-like column, gracefully thrusting uphill at an incredible speed. It was the Megamicro, the longest ski de fond race with a start and finish in Switzerland, 75km which the leaders would complete in just over 3 hours! If you get embroiled in a race, you should still be able to continue along the edge of the piste.

Cross the road at Le Gardot and continue up a long rising combe with enclosing forest on either side, past three farms to a steep rise to a col (1,200m) and the large auberge gîte of **Vieux Chatelu**, Grande-Combe-Chateleu, 25790 Les Gras. Tel: 81.67.11.59. (M. S/C). The piste runs above the auberge then crosses the road. If the day is clear it is worth a diversion to the top of Monte Chatelu (1,301m). The trail (green) to this forks right just a short way along the GTJ and rises to a col with the summit just a little further.

Now you encounter the first real descent of the GTJ - a long gentle run below the slopes of Mont Chatelu into a delightful little valley which opens into a combe with the hamlet of Nid du Fol on the right (road crossings, caution). There is a steep ascent through forest, below the even steeper slopes of the slim crest which marks the frontier, to join another trail at Les Cerneaux, the piste system of Les Seignes. (At the junction the trail right drops to the village of Les Gras 2km.) Straight on enter another combe with the hamlet of **Les Seignes**

(1,045m) on the right. A road right leads through the hamlet 1km to the gîte of **Le Grand Mont**, 25790 Les Gras. Tel: 81.68.82.10. (M).

Keep to the left edge of the combe which rises gently and gives views across to the Rochers du Cerf. Keep alongside a road to cross it near Chalet Charopey. The trail goes below the first chalet then rises above the second to reach the Swiss frontier, marked by stubby posts.

The next section along the rising combe was unpisted when my party passed, but marker posts show the way. An attractive forest road with a steep ascent leads up the Combe la Cornée to a clearing at its top. Here is a junction of trails as we join another piste system. Right is the GTJ Liaison from Montbenoit. Our route leaves the piste system and climbs left up a steep forested slope on a well graded track to 1,250m, before running down a long gentle combe, the Chez le Brandt. The track runs into the centre of the combe to pass the large farm and sawmill of Joli Mas, where a poem on the farm wall evokes the spirit of mountain beauty and companionship. Pass Petit Brandt to gain the far side of the combe. Note the cave shaft a few yards right - the Grotte de Brandt, which has a vertical depth of around 250ft.

Reach **Grands Cernets** (1,154m), Auberge des Cernets, 2126 les Verrières/NE, Switzerland. Tel: 19.41.38.66.12.65. (M. (S/C). There is also a Centre Sportif where accommodation may be available.

We encountered a Swiss border patrol here, friendly but firm. Our passports were inspected and the usual questions asked. 'Have you any whisky, cigarettes or uncooked meats?' Our packs were heavy enough without such luxuries.

Don't go as far as the crossroads in **Petits Cernets** (Gîte) but turn right by a small lane. The GTJ lies parallel to the lane, but if it is unpisted you can join it past La Rossel, by the French frontier, marked by the familiar chunky black posts poking out of the snow. This section may be tracked but unpisted. Almost level going through forest reaches a broad clearing on the slopes of Montagne du Larmont, the hill above Pontarlier which marks the end of this particular Jura crest. Descend the clearing past the Granges d'Agneaux.

The ensuing descent is long and entertaining, the first real test of technique. The track zig-zags but enough speed is gained to worry novices, with a final steep swoop into the frontier village of **Les Verrières** 915m (Gîte: 'Le Chalet', Hotel restaurant but no shop). Take skis off to walk right, past the customs post into France. If the trail is pisted look for its continuation on the left, where it crosses the valley floor and runs alongside the railway. If not, continue through the village, turn left by the church (note the fine colourful mosaic on its dome). Turn left again and cross a level crossing. Go straight up to

Between Le Tillau and Les Fourgs the GTJ is not always machine pisted after snowfall.

join the pisted GTJ, or turn right along a track which joins the GTJ a little further.

Follow the valley side west to a zig-zag past the Granges de Largillat. Here the trail ascends steeply through forest to a shelf at its top. A sign warns skiers coming the other way of the dangers of the steep descent. The GTJ may be unpisted here and could be confusing. The official way lies just inside the forest, parallel and just below its top edge, but many skiers ascend the combe above the trees, cross a wire fence then another fence on the right to zig-zag up to a lane, which is followed left to a junction with the official route. The road continues up another zig-zag to the fine new building of the **Auberge le Tillau** (1,170m), Le Mont-des-Verrières-de-Joux, 25300 Pontarlier. Tel: 81.69.46.72. This is very popular, renowned for its fine meals, and advance booking is advised.

The next stretch crosses a fine upland of gentle hills with a mix of trees. It forms part of the extensive Les Fourgs piste system, but was unpisted on my crossing. From behind Le Tillau, cross the slopes rightwards to the plateau top. Gentle undulations ensue, past clearings and a road to enter forest. After a zig-zag descent past the Granges des Combes on the left, reach the farm of **Les Granges Bailly**, Les Fourgs, 25300 Pontarlier. Tel: 81.69.40.62. (S/C). This is less likely to be booked up than the more sophisticated gîtes, as the French prefer to have their meals prepared!

Just after the Granges go on a road for 400 yards and just after a bend fork right on the edge of a wood to enter the wide open bleak area around Les Fourgs; on a poor day its description as 'Little Siberia' seems very appropriate. The trail crosses another road below Les Granges Berard and continues to the top end of **Les Fourgs** (1,100m). Where the GTJ meets the road is a large restaurant gîte auberge **L'Orgière**, La Combe du Mouillan, Les Fourgs, 25300 Pontarlier. Tel: 81.69.41.09. (M. S/C). This gîte is renowned for its husky dogs and tours with dog sleds can be arranged.

Les Fourgs is a long straggling village with several shops. There are other gîtes in the area and plenty of other accommodation.

A recommended gîte is at Haut Joux, about 1km left along the road at the north end of the village. Fork left to the gîte - Le Centre Nordique 'La Babaude' (1,137m) (M. S/C).

The GTJ runs around the top edge of the village on a broad major pisted trail. It keeps below a wooded slope on the edge of the wide open snow bowl until the forest closes in. Keep straight on where a trail breaks right, then keep right at a fork. (Orange markers on the left fork are misleading - follow the signed trail towards Les Hôpitaux and Jougne.) A steep straight descent drops to a flat valley floor to an Information Centre and car access at La Beridale. Turn left off the road and follow the trail. Les Hôpitaux Vieux is the village on the right. The GTJ comes close to a the road at **Les Hôpitaux Neufs**, a larger busy village on a main road, with full shopping facilities. The trail skirts well above the village to a junction where the black piste rises again into the forest. Turn right 100 yards to join the road. There is a Casino supermarket not far down on the right.

The nearest gîte is a further kilometre at the neighbouring village of **Jougne.** Gîte dÉtape Chez Polon, Jougne, 25370 Les Hôpitaux Neufs. Tel: 81.49.12.70. Jougne is an attractive fortified town.

GTJ
LES HÔPITAUX NEUFS to LA CURE (LES ROUSSES)
77.50km   3/4 days

Maps: Ski de Fond Massif du Jura Sheets 3,4 and 5. 1:25,000
Didier & Richard Sheet 33 'Au Coeur du Jura' and 34 'Jura Sud'. 1:50,000.

	KM.	ACC.KM.	
Les Hôpitaux Neufs	0.00	0.00	
La Boissaude	8.50	8.50	Gîte
Mouthe	11.00	19.50	Gîtes
Chaux-Neuve	6.00	25.50	
Prés d'Haut	6.00	31.50	Gîte
Chapelle des Bois	7.00	38.50	
Chalet Flacan	20.00	58.50	Gîte (1km)
Bois d'Amont	5.50	64.00	Gîte
La Cure	10.50	74.50	
Les Rousses	3.00	77.50	

Les Hôpitaux derives its name from a monastery around which the village grew. This section follows well pisted trails throughout, using piste systems of some of the most popular ski centres in the Jura. There should be little route finding difficulties - just follow the orange signs. The trail rises onto the main secondary crest of the Jura, with Mont d'Or the highest point at 1,464m, a worthy diversion. The route criss-crosses this broad forested crest to end along the flat valley of the Orbe to Les Rousses. Fortunately accommodation is plentiful, as this is a very busy section during the high season, but it is wise to pre-book.

From the upper, southern end of Les Hôpitaux, go along the road a short way towards Jougne to a lane which branches right across the hillside. Follow this and the trail forks right to pass above the top of a teleski and joins a more direct alternative route from the centre of the village. Pass two further ski-lifts which serve a nursery area for downhill novices then descend gently to a large ski car park above the thriving holiday resort of **Metabief**. Numerous modern chalets testify to its popularity as a winter resort, with an excellent downhill piste system on the steep northern and eastern slopes of Le Morond and Mont d'Or.

After a level kilometre, shared with other ski de fond pistes, the GTJ goes left, uphill to traverse the steep wooded slopes of Le Morond on a system of forest lanes. Pass the Chalet de Paradis and join a road to reach another parking area at the foot of ski-lifts on the upper west slopes of Le Morond (1,418m). There is a CAF Chalet du Gros Morond 1km up the combe. The ski-lift is useful if you intend to make a diversion to visit the summit plateau of Mont d'Or, for it takes

Mont d'Or is a rewarding short diversion from the main trail.

you right to the crest. You can then traverse the undulating ridge, taking great care not to go too close to the huge cornices on the eastern edge. At the far end is the Swiss CAS refuge (open weekends), where a piste is joined which goes right back across the mountain at a lower level to the Chalet Boissaude. If the weather is good and you have a couple of hours to spare, this diversion will reward you with views of the Alps and a highlight of the whole trip.

However, the GTJ continues from the foot of the ski-lift along an undulating route past the **Chalet la Barthelette** (1,200m) ARTMO 25370 Les Longevilles-Mont d'Or. Tel: 81.49.90.95. (M. S/C). This refuge lies a short distance below the GTJ on the right. Another 1.5km along the trail is the more popular overnight stop - the ferme auberge **Chalet la Boissaude** (dortoirs) Rochejean, 25370 Les Hôpitaux Neufs. Tel: 81.39.17.35. (M) Booking advisable.

The plateau hereabouts is a veritable crossroads, for it hosts not only the GTJ and the local ski pistes system, but the TJS and the route along the Crêtes, which branch south into Switzerland and the other side of the Val de Joux. The GTJ keeps along the northern edge of the plateau, delightful ski country.

From La Boissaude the trail, more or less coincident with the electricity wires, descends to cross a road at Les Granges Raguin, a junction of pistes. An open combe is followed and over its top in the forest, the piste circuit bends away and the GTJ sweeps on, to descend past the Grange Vannot and through another two clearings to reach the edge of the plateau. A forest road is joined to provide an easy descent of the steep hillside to the floor of the long combe of the Doubs and the attractive village of **Mouthe** (shops, accommodation). Near the village is the Gîte Communale 'La Source du Doubs' 25240 Mouthe. Tel: 81.69.27.41. (M). 2km north-east is the Gîte Communale de Sarrageois and at least two other gîtes lie within 3km. Mouthe lies at the centre of an extensive ski piste system which covers the valley and the forested hills on either side.

From the southern end of the village, the trail keeps left of the road to Petite Chaux, where it goes sharp left into a tiny parallel side combe. This rises to a shelf which is traversed to descend to a road just above Chaux-Neuve. Pass the foot of teleskis and continue in the same line up another shallow combe. **Chatelblanc** lies 1km north-west -Gîte d'Étape, Le Castel Blanc, 25240 Chatelblanc. Tel: 81.69.24.56. (M).

The GTJ now leaves the combe to traverse the forested upland of Le Mont Noir, a very attractive section of the trip. Pass the farm of Les Serments and just over a low col the trail turns left to wind up dense forest which now predominates for several kilometres. Once on the plateau the trail is interesting as it winds around small hillocks to join the ski piste system from Chapelle-des-Bois. A branch right goes to the popular overnight gîte of **Les Prés d'Haut** Les Ruines 39460 Foncine-le-Haut. Tel: 84.51.93.18. (M. S/C). The gîte is situated on a hilltop clearing, 4km from the nearest road, a charming situation.

The trail continues to serpent a way in the forest before descent to an open combe, past Nordances to the small village of **Chapelle-des-Bois** at 1,080m assured of a good snow cover for much of the ski season. It is said that its winter snowfall is comparable with that on the summit of Mont Blanc. The village lies in a small bowl with the very steep scarp on its south-west, the edge of the Risoux plateau, dominated by the Roche Champion. On the other side of the scarp are the numerous ski trails of the Swiss Risoux and Les Rousses. However, a suitable easy route up the barrier is only available 5km further along the floor of the combe towards Bellefontaine. Chapelle-des-Bois is renowned for its ski de fond centre, situated at the northern entry to the village. The centre runs courses for beginners and also organizes ski tours of a week or two weeks duration along the routes outlined in this book. There is the possibility of overnight accommodation at the centre.

The GTJ officially branches right just before entering Chapelle-des-

Bois and makes a long semicircle towards Bellefontaine. There is a shorter trail along the floor of the combe from Chapelle-des-Bois, to the same point. The GTJ keeps just above the road to Chez Michel and bends right to undulate through forest. Cross a minor road and near the Chalet des Voiles bear left away from the road to make a pleasant descent into the head of the **Combe de Morbier** Gîte at La Combette 39400 Morbier. Tel: 84.33.27.23. Lovers of cheese will recognise the name, for Morbier, with its distinctive stripe, can usually be bought throughout the area. Leave the combe almost immediately with a stiff ascent left of the Bois de Chaux Mourant. A shelf on the other side lies above the village of **Bellefontaine** (Possibility of accommodation at the OCCAJ holiday centre. Tel: 84.33.19.86).

Cross the road which links Bellefontaine to Chapelle-des-Bois. The entrance to the piste system of Risoux starts here. (This point can be gained by a shorter direct route from Chapelle-des-Bois by traversing the floor of the combe. Leave the GTJ at Chez Michel to pass the edge of the Lacs des Mortes.)

The GTJ rises up a forest road which mounts the scarp onto the tormented relief of the Risoux plateau, a region of densely forested little knolls and hollows. The piste system uses the maze of forest lanes. Just follow the orange signs. Fork left at the Chalet des Ministres (a spartan backpackers' shelter) and 2km further note the track left to the popular gîte d'étape, the **Chalet Gailland (Flacan)** (1,232m) Foret du Risoux, 39220 Les Rousses. Tel: 84.60.94.13. (M. S/C). 700m from the GTJ.

The main trail passes the edge of a broad clearing then comes to the edge of the eastern scarp, which is skied down to the village of Bois d'Amont (1,070m) which lies close to the Swiss frontier in the combe of the Orbe, which extends as the Val de Joux, a fine skiing area. Gîte d'Accueil, 39220 Bois d'Amont. Tel: 84.60.92.62.

The trail follows the edge of the flat combe, keeping on French ground as it traverses below the road, parallel to the frontier and past the downhill ski area of the Noirmont. The Lac des Rousses lies to the right in the floor of the valley and a closer look can be obtained by taking the parallel piste intriguingly named 'Little Lapland'. Cross a road, which marks the nearest point to Les Rousses, to rise up the Crêt des Landes, a slight spur in the floor of the broad combe, and reach the frontier village of **La Cure** just to the left. La Cure is the terminus to the mountain railway from Nyon on the shores of Lake Geneva, and is convenient for a rail return to the start of the GTJ via Neuchâtel and Le Locle.

Three kilometres right is the larger village of **Les Rousses**, the metropolis of the area with shopping, tourist information and other facilities. It is a good opportunity to stock up at a supermarket. In winter Les Rousses throbs with crowds as it is one of the major downhill ski centres of the Jura as well as a popular ski de fond centre.

GTJ
LA CURE (LES ROUSSES) to GIRON
44km   2/3 days

Maps: Ski de Fond Massif du Jura Sheets 5 and 6. 1:25,000.
Didier & Richard Sheet 34 Jura Sud. 1:50,000.

	KM.	ACC.KM.	
La Cure	0.00		
Chalet de la Frasse	7.00	7.00	Gîte
Lajoux	10.00	17.00	Gîte
Les Adrets	6.00	23.00	Gîte
Le Berbois	10.00	33.00	Gîte
Ref. Tamiset	3.00	36.00	Refuge
Giron	8.00	44.00	Foyer de Fond

(Les Rousses lies 3km from La Cure)

The flat topped wedge of forested crest which this stage follows is punctuated in its centre by a broad upland combe with the village of Lajoux at its centre. The final section from the head of Bellecombe to Giron is one of the most rewarding on the trip, with opportunity to bag a worthwhile summit. Once again it is a very well pisted section with a multitude of ski trails radiating from various popular centres. It is almost certain to be busy but there is plenty of accommodation on or close to the route. Shops at Les Rousses, Lajoux and a tiny one at Giron, or use shops in the neighbouring villages.

The GTJ descends from La Cure to the head of the deep valley of La Chaille. On the right 1km down the valley is a Youth Hostel at le Bief de la Chaille. There is a change of topography here, as the broad flat valley with Les Rousses is left behind. Now there are rows of parallel forested hills with deep narrow valleys between. The valley ahead lies on the right of the steep ended Montagne des Tuffes (1,418m), another of the scattered downhill ski areas around Les Rousses. Enter the valley below ski-lifts and parking areas.

The ski-lifts could be utilised to reach the summit of the hill, which marks the end of the lengthy Forêt du Massacre. A forest road zig-zags down and left from the top into a combe with the foresters' shelter of Les Tuffes. A more sophisticated overnight stop can be found at the **Loge de Beauregard** 39220 Prémanon. Tel: 84.60.77.14. (M). From Les Tuffes the forest trail undulates past the Chalet Forestière du Massacre (no overnight - locked) to the crossroads at Carrefour le Goulet where the official GTJ joins.

The GTJ follows the valley from the foot of the ski-lifts, close to the main road. A road branches right to **Prémanon** a small village and ski de fond centre which lies on a shelf at the head of the parallel range of hills. There is a gîte - Chez Fofo, 39220, Prémanon. Tel: 84.60.04.51. (M. S/C). The village is dominated by the steep rock prow of Mont Fier.

At the road junction is the École National de Ski. The GTJ continues, right of the road, up the combe past yet more downhill ski-lifts. After 3km from the école, the route rises up the flank of the forest along a zig-zag forest lane. Pass the popular gîte, **Chalet de la Frasse** (1,293m) Forêt du Massacre. 39310 Lamoura. Tel: 84.42.64.81. (M. S/C); This is an old chalet in an attractive situation, owned by the commune of Lamoura. The trail rises to the Carrefour le Goulet to meet the alternative route, turn right and mount steadily to a col. Just before the col a path is signed right to Crêt Pela, (1,495m) the highest summit hereabouts and worth the half hour diversion if the weather is good. The steep slopes on the other side of the Crêt Pela are used by a host of downhill ski pistes.

Back on the trail a long descent shoots out of the forest onto the edge of the broad upland combe to join the piste system which radiates from Lajoux. The GTJ here resembles a six lane motorway and joins the road at the top edge of **Lajoux**, a long straggly village. Near the GTJ is the large modern holiday OCCAJ chalet with a gîte d'étape almost in its roof. Tel: 84.41.23.00.

You will have passed several trails signed to **Lamoura**, a neighbouring ski village quite close to the GTJ and offering gîte accommodation at Le Fournets, 39310 Lamoura. Tel: 84.41.25.27. There are other gîtes close by.

From Lajoux the trail crosses the combe to La Bisse and traverses above a steep valley to enter the long upland combe of Bellecombe. On the left is the gîte **Les Adrets**, 39310 Bellecombe. Tel: 84.41.65.82. (M. S/C).

The broad floor of Bellecombe makes easy skiing, past the gîte of **Chez le Gris** and the farm of Bellecombe. The combe becomes narrower as the forested sides close in. At Les Closettes the trail curls around the base of the **Crêt au Merle** (1,448m) to a junction of trails at a monument. This lies at the head of a very deep side combe whose presence has been glimpsed through the trees. The summit of Crêt au Merle is only a short diversion to the right and is well worth the effort, especially if you do not intend to climb the neighbouring and more difficult Crêt Chalam. Fine views are obtained of the highest peaks of the Jura across the deep valley of Valserine.

Back at the junction, right leads to the gîte **Le Berbois** AGAD, 39370 La Pesse. Tel: 84.42.72.41. (M. S/C). The village of **La Pesse** lies 3km further and has more gîte accommodation close by.

The GTJ keeps left at the junction to rise gently through dense forest along the northern slopes of the **Crêt Chalam.**

Crêt Chalam (1,545m), the highest summit encountered on the GTJ and well worth the effort involved in its ascent if you have a couple of hours to spare. The GTJ rises to a col. Before this col is reached a summer track goes left and this is the way to the peak although it may be difficult to spot in deep unpisted snow. An alternative even steeper route goes straight up from the col and both routes meet on a shoulder where the final pyramid of the Crêt Chalam is seen. This may be tricky in poor snow conditions as the slope is steep, and could pose an avalanche risk in some circumstances. Descend the same way to the GTJ.

Just over the col there is a clearing and a track right to the unguarded **Refuge Tamiset**. This is a simple shelter for backpackers and although locked, the key should be found over the door. A night here combined with the ascent of the Crêt Chalam, is a fitting climax to the trip, although a relatively hefty overnight fee is requested by the commune.

Pass through a gap and the trail descends along the steep edge of the plateau with views across the valley of the Semine to row upon row of forested hills. After a fine descent the views are sacrificed again to the ubiquitous forest as we enter the complex area of ski pistes which radiate from Giron in the rumpled plateau of the Forêt de Champ-fromier. Pass a linking trail which joins from La Pesse and continue along the western edge of the plateau. Pistes join from the left at regular intervals. A few minutes along the third trail on the left lies another unguarded forester's chalet, the Chalet Cottin. Continue along the GTJ towards Giron. There is a rapid, fairly steep descent, on the right, or an easier alternative a little further along.

The unguarded Refuge de Tamiset lies below the Crêt Chalam on the GTJ.

Giron is a small village with a foyer de ski de fond which offers accommodation, and marks the end of the GTJ for most people. If there is enough snow it is possible to ski quite a long way towards the valley above Montagnes, otherwise the ski centre will advise on transport to Bellegarde, the nearest town and main railway station.

The GTJ does continue to traverse the **Bugey**, but it is necessary to cross the very deep valley of St. Germaine de Joux. You can get a navette or taxi from Giron to the start of the trail again at Le Poizat.

THE TRAVERSE OF THE SWISS JURA (TJS)

149km   7/9 days

The TJS is the Swiss equivalent of the French GTJ but is much less popular and less likely to be machine pisted.

Maps: K & F Wanderkarte des Jura. 1:50,000 Sheets 4,5 and 6.

	KM.	ACC.KM.
Saignelégier	0.00	0.00
La-Chaux-de-Fonds	26.00	26.00
La Brévine	26.00	52.00
Les Cernets	15.00	67.00
Les Verrières	3.00	70.00
La Côte-aux-Fées	6.00	76.00
Les Hôpitaux Neufs	15.00	91.00
Le Pont	22.00	113.00
Col de la Givrine	36.00	149.00

There are ski trails on the upland plateau of Franches-Montagnes, west of Délémont, where the altitude reaches almost 1,000m, but the proximity of roads, villages and other habitations renders the skiing rather ordinary. The trail skirts Saignelégier, Le Noirmont and La Ferrière to traverse the rolling hills between Chaux-de-Fonds and Vue des Alpes.

A recommended starting point for a tour is **Chaux-de-Fonds**, the largest town in the area, easily reached by public transport. Between the town and the highest Jura crest lies a secondary lower crest which the TJS follows. Either traverse the crest of La Sagne or the trail on its north-west slopes. Views from the crest towards the Tête de Ran and Mont Racine across the flat intervening combe, are very attractive. The crest narrows to cross a gap and road above Les Ponts de Marcel, then the trail descends into the long flat bottomed combe on the right to **La Brévine** (Gîte). The crest which bounds the combe to its north forms the frontier and hosts the GTJ.

From La Brévine there is a choice of route. The shorter (15km) follows the floor of the combe, close to a road at first to Chincoul

Backpackers ascend the combe towards Mont d'Or.

Dessous, near the valley head. Forested terrain is then traversed right to L'Endroit. Shortly after a trail forks left to descend into **Grands Cernets** (Gîte). **Petits Cernets** is a little further.

The alternative (17km) is more wooded, more varied and more interesting as it keeps to the higher ground which borders the valley to its south. From La Brévine the trail rises through clearings to Les Fontanettes. Reach Le Cernil (Auberge) in a clearing where a road crosses the crest. Continue in dense forest to Le Haut des Côtes to Les Cernets.

The GTJ is met at Les Cernets, but the TJS keeps to trails in Switzerland to gain the deep, busy main road/rail valley. Descend on the left of the main road, then cross it to make the final swoosh to the valley. Cross the railway and main road to reach the Swiss **Les Verrières.**

At the eastern end of the village a forest lane climbs the very steep southern slopes of the valley onto the plateau of Mont des Verrières. Cross the undulating plateau to **La Côte-aux-Fées.** The trail keeps close to the French frontier which is crossed at the road between L'Auberson and Les Fourgs, to join the extensive pisted trail system of **Les Fourgs** (Gîtes).

There is no need to go into the village, as from the frontier, there is a

The Refuge des Pralets stands near the junction of trails at the head of the Combe d'Amburnex.

more direct piste to Les Hôpitaux. Here the TJS joins the GTJ which is followed to the high plateau beyond Mont d'Or. Pass the Chalet Boissaude (Gîte) and the Granges Raguin where the trail bears south to drop from the plateau into a deep little valley past the foresters' cabin of La Pisserette. Cross the hill to reach **Le Pont.**

The continuation of the route is as described in the description of the Traverse of the Crêtes - a superb traverse of the upland combes on the shoulder of Mont Tendre, the long Combe d'Amburnex, to finish over the forested hills to the **Col de la Givrine.**

TRAVERSE OF THE CRÊTES

237km   12/14 days

The most demanding of the traverses - and the most rewarding for the experienced mountain skier - takes the highest most easterly crest of the Jura from Weissenstein (1,285m) to Bellegarde. Much of the route lies close to the summer High Route although easier skiing is often sought on the shelves below its crest.

Technically the skiing is easy, yet it is no place for novices. Many parts are unlikely to be pisted and good map reading is necessary. Likewise good judgement is required in bad weather. Snow conditions can vary enormously and plans may need to be altered to cater for too much or too little snow! The area seems much wilder than in summer and the air is generally much clearer giving continual views to the alps. At first with the Eiger, Monch and Jungfrau dominating the scene, then gradually Mont Blanc and the Aiguilles draw nearer to become familiar companions.

The complete traverse is long and rarely done as a whole. The route is more easily done in sections and parts can be combined with the GTJ or TJS to make a satisfying circuit.

Accommodation is more difficult to find than in summer as many upland farms are abandoned for the winter. There are several CAS and CAF chalets dotted along the route, fine if you are a member and have a key, but most are only open at weekends or if a party is using them. Non-members can stay overnight at very reasonable cost if they are open, but will have to prepare their own meals. Other accommodation is found along the way in small hotels, ferme auberges, or gîtes. Most of the hotels have cheap dortoirs (Touristenlagen). Pre-booking is recommended at busy times perhaps by phoning ahead along the route when conditions allow an accurate assessment of the day's stage.

Guided parties regularly traverse sections of the route - for more information see addresses on page 183.

The tourist office at Neuchâtel can supply a booklet which lists overnight accommodation along the JHR, but it does not indicate those closed for winter. In the text I have indicated some certain overnight stops.

The best time for the traverse is spring, when there is less chance of encountering deep snow. If you are lucky you will be able to run off-piste with skis just sinking enough to prevent that runaway feel. After prolonged heavy snow the route is impractical. Perhaps the best aim is to link any accessible pistes along the route, but to take in as many of the higher summits as possible. Note that summit crests can be icy or windblown into sastrugi which makes unpleasant skiing. Low lying sections may be snow free.

Note: Distances given are very approximate and will vary according to choice of route. Detours to incorporate various summits are not included.

WEISSENSTEIN to VUE DES ALPES
60km   3/4 days

Maps: K & F Wanderkarte des Jura. 1:50,000 Sheets 3 and 4.

		KM.	ACC.KM.
Solothurn			
Oberdorf	620m	4.00	
Weissenstein	1,284m	5.00	Start of ski traverse
Ober Grenchenberg	1,348m	9.00	9.00
La Rochette (CAS)	1,300m	10.00	19.00
Sonceboz	650m	9.50	28.50
Le Chasseral	1,607m	13.00	41.50
Les Bugnenets	1,091m	6.00	47.50
Vue des Alpes	1,283m	13.00	60.50

Reach the Kurhaus Hotel Weissenstein from Oberdorf station by chair-lift if it is running, or by a road which zig-zags steeply up the hillside. The flat playeau top of the mountain makes a fine easy start to the route, rising to the base of Hasenmatt (1,444m). This can be bypassed on the north by Althussli to regain the main crest beyond. The safest ski route leaves the crest here to traverse right round the steep slopes to Stallberg, on a small col. Descend the line of a summer road into the base of a valley which is climbed steeply to the plateau of Ober Grenchenberg. (SAC Clubhaus Grenchenberg lies nearby.)

From here you could continue along the line of the summer High Route across the plateau of Montagne de Romont to Plagne (possibility of accommodation) and Frinvillier, but a more certain ski route lies on the more northerly crest, Le Montoz.

From Ober Grenchenberg follow close below the northern edge of the combe to Langschmang and ascend onto the edge of a broad undulating plateau which comprises the summit of Le Montoz. There are several upland farms and SAC-Clubhaus La Rochette, below the summit of the same name 1,327m. Continue west along the narrowing plateau past Mét de Werdt which lies above a deep combe to the south. From the western rim of the combe begin a long steep descent, most easily by a zig-zag track to Pierre Pertuis where the road is joined and skis taken off. 2km right along this is the village of Tavannes (Hotels), 2km left is the smaller village of Sonceboz, in the deep valley of La Suze, which runs parallel to the bounding ridge of Le Chasseral, the highest summit of the area.

Cross the river and walk up a spur past Cernil du Bas. Hopefully it will not be long before you encounter snow on the north-facing slopes. Join a rough lane which zig-zags up the hillside to cut through a subsidiary ridge at a defile - the Pont des Anabaptistes, to gain the long upland combe which runs below and parallel to the ridge of Le Chasseral. The easiest ski route is along this gently rising combe, so typical of this section of the Jura. There are possibilities of overnight accommodation on the ridge at the SAC Jurahaus, or over the other side at the Prés d'Orvin.

If the day is good then continue along the ridge to the summit of Le Chasseral (1,607m) with breathtaking alpine views. Descend past the closed hotel and gain the combe below right. The alternative is to ski the long combe from Pont des Anabaptistes to the Petit Chasseral at its head. You can gain the main summit easily from here or traverse the shelf into the combe below the hotel.

To the west is a low crest with downhill ski runs through the forest on the other side. The easiest way is by a summer road which runs round the northern end of the crest and zig-zags down to Les Bugnenets. (Hotel restaurant.) (Other accommodation is available in St. Imier, the town in the valley just over the subsidiary crest to the north.) Here we join the long piste system of the Pays de Neuchâtel, which should ensure speedy progress along the plateaux of Joux du Plâne. (CAS Cabane de la Joux du Plâne and another nearby - CAS Cabane Mont d'Amin.) The pistes continue on the broad combe below the long thin forested ridge of Mont d'Amin to a very busy main road and bustling hotel at the Vue des Alpes. This is a popular downhill ski centre.

The large, attractive open-plan town of La Chaux-de-Fonds lies six kilometres to the north, with full shopping facilities and plenty of accommodation.

VUE DES ALPES to JOUGNE
63km   3/4 days

Maps: K & F Wanderkarte des Jura. 1:50,000 Sheet 4 and 5.

		KM.	ACC.KM.
Vue des Alpes	1,283m	0.00	0.00
La Tourne	1,129m	12.50	12.50
Noraigue	720m	8.00	20.50
Ferme Robert	972m	2.00	22.50
Les Cluds	1,210m	21.50	44.00
Les Rasses	1,188m	3.00	47.00
Ste. Croix	1,066m	3.00	50.00
Col de l'Aiguillon	1,320m	5.00	55.00
Jougne	1,012m	8.00	63.00

A popular well tracked piste starts from the huge car park just north of Vue des Alpes and runs up the combe parallel with a road and the low forested crest. A branch left leads to the very busy Hotel Tête de Ran in 2.5km (Restaurant, dortoirs). This serves a popular downhill ski area on the steep eastern slopes of the mountain.

The piste along the combe continues to rise below the main crest, then after a short descent past the chalet of Les Neigeux (drinks) rises to a low col on a shoulder. The machine piste turns here to make its return - we continue down a shallow valley, then along a rising track through the forest to a low col on the crest. (Close by is the CAS Cabane Les Pradières.) Across the undulating plateau is the summit of Mont Racine 1,439m. After a kilometre along the ridge regain the shelf on the west. This could be followed without the climb to Mont Racine. Round the head of a steep combe drop steeply to La Tourne (Restaurant). Descend a long gentle combe south-west to reach a main road at the edge of a strange flat upland valley, the plain of Les Bieds, which has been a landmark along this section and appears in winter like a white lake. The crest on the other side of the plain is host to the TJS ski traverse.

From the edge of the plain is a dramatic view into the deep gorges of L'Areuse with the horseshoe cirque of Creux du Van opposite. In the valley base is the village of Noraigue which will probably be snow free. Walk down the road a short way to where a steep path branches left

163

The upland shelf which runs below the Tête de Ran is usually machine pisted.

through the forest into the village. (Hotel and dortoir accommodation.)

Take the road across the river to the Ferme Robert which sits at the base of the impressive Creux du Van. (Restaurant, dortoir.) The cirque is one of the most dramatic sights of the Jura, especially when its vertical cliffs are decked with ice and rimmed with huge cornices.

The next part of the route is hard work - a steep ascent up the zig-zags in the forested side wall of the combe to its edge at a col between La Chaille and Signal de Lessy. This is the north-eastern end of a broad plateau area, very popular in winter with a network of trails. The machine pistes do not quite penetrate to the edge of the Creux du Van, but are soon joined to make easy going to Les Rasses.

From the col on the edge of the cirque climb a shallow combe past Le Grand Vy. We have joined the main summer High Route and follow it more or less for a while. If the weather is poor and views lacking, then continue above Le Grand Vy over a slight col and descend the combe on the other side past Baronne to join pisted ski trails. However, if the day is clear then a diversion to the summit of Le Soliat (1,463m) is one of the highlights of the trip. Ski along the rim of the Creux du Van, keeping on the safe side of a small stone wall which pokes through the blown snow. The other side is heavily corniced above sheer cliffs. Several projections allow the awesome view to be appreciated. From the summit you can turn left and ski down a slight combe with a steeper drop to La Baronne, or continue along the edge of the cirque to the deserted farm of Le Soliat, whence a track descends gently through forest to gain the machine pisted trails of Nouvelles Censieres, at first along a combe then a broad shelf on the western side of the plateau. At various points along the trail are boards which show the layout of the pistes. There is a possibility of accommodation at the Ski Club de Couvet (weekends), which lies a short distance down the road from Le Couvent, and more certain accommodation at the auberge Les Planes.

Another alternative is to keep to the trails along the top of the plateau, past La Bolene, La Grange Neuve and La Roguire to join the other trails for the final stretch to Les Cluds (Restaurant, dortoir).

A third alternative from Baronne lies down a slight valley straight ahead. On the left is the Crêt Teni, a small hill with the SAC Cabane Perrenoud on its summit. A night here is a rewarding experience especially if clear visibility allows the sunrise over the Alps to be appreciated. As with most of these CAS cabins, it is only guardianed at weekends. The valley joins pisted trails past Les Rochat (Restaurant) to join the other trials at La Combax.

A defile leads onto a broad shelf, the Balcon du Jura, which is a major ski de fond highway past Les Cluds to Les Rasses (Hotels, dortoirs), the starting point of the trail system. Les Rasses lies at the

Cornices above the impressive void of the Creux du Van. Caution is essential - note the hesitant figure top left.

Sunrise over the Alps from SAC Cabane Perrenoud. Lac de Neuchâtel in the foreground. Eiger, Mönch and Jungfrau in the centre background.

foot of a downhill ski area whose lifts reach almost to the top of Le Chasseron (1,607m).

For the experienced, the traverse of Le Chasseron makes yet another alternative. The trail branches from the main shelf about 2 kilometres before Les Cluds, at La Cruchaude and rises onto the summit ridge. There is a restaurant on top (Dortoirs). A descent can be made below the subsidiary summits of Petites Roches and Le Cochet, utilising parts of the easier downhill pistes, to reach the bustling village of Ste. Croix. (Hotels, Youth Hostels, shops, train link to Yverdon.)

At the top end of the village a lane goes left up a combe to La Gîte Dessous on the crest of a small ridge. Rise up a broad gentle shelf past La Gîte Dessus to the frontier Col de l'Aiguillon (1,320m) below the steep craggy slopes of Aiguilles de Balmes.

Several options are now open. You can go straight down the valley of the Jougnena, past a small backpackers' shelter, the Abri de Queue, where a trail rises right onto the machined pistes above Jougne. Or follow the forest road right for two kilometres down several bends to a right-hand hairpin very close to the French frontier. Here go left for a few yards to join the machine piste. Follow it down

166

right for one kilometre to the squalid but cosy **Refuge de la Joux**. This is a simple shelter ideal for backpackers: note that the situation for backpackers is much easier from this point along the traverse. The pistes then lead into Jougne (Hotels, dortoirs, gîte d'étape, shops).

A third alternative from the Col de l'Aiguillon in good weather is to incorporate the shapely summit of Le Suchet (1,588m), a commanding isolated viewpoint, but a steep climb on skis. Descent can be made on the south-west slopes to a col at La Poyette, where a track leads over Bel Costa, past La Paigrette (CAF Refuge) to the head of a teleski installation above the little ski village of Entre les Fourgs (Hotels, dortoirs). You can ski on pistes north-east to the Abri de Queue to link onto the tracks above Jougne, or reach Jougne by road.

The deep valley which is one of the major through routes of the Jura is a convenient point to break the traverse. Vallorbe, a main line railway town lies a few kilometres to the south, with a good train service back to Solothurn.

JOUGNE to LA GIVRINE
60.50km   3/4 days

Maps: K & F Carte Speciale du Jura. 1:50,000 Sheets 5 & 6 or
D & R Au Coeur du Jura. 1:50,000 Sheet 33 (This does not
include the Swiss section over Monte Tendre).

		KM.	ACC.KM.
Jougne	1,012m	0.00	0.00
La Boissaude	1,214m	10.00	10.00
Les Charbonnières	1,008m	12.00	22.00
Le Pont	1,008m	1.50	23.50
Monte Tendre	1,679m	11.00	34.50
Col du Marchairuz	1,447m	7.00	41.50
La Givrine	1,208m	19.00	60.50

This stage is more or less coincident with the TJS and the stretch from Col du Mollendruz to La Givrine is usually machine pisted.

From Jougne ascend the slopes of Mont Ramey to the west of the village either by a lane or close to the teleski. You soon join a ski de fond trail which ascends gently right above the teleskis then descends to the top of teleskis above Les Hôpitaux. Join the GTJ left to the busy parking above the popular ski centre of Metabief.

This is one of the few downhill ski areas of the Jura which compares with the minor Alpine ski resorts. The very steep east and north slopes of Mont d'Or have a selection of excellent downhill pistes.

You can either follow the GTJ which rises through the trees to pass the Chalet de Paradis in a slight valley, or reach the same point by taking the ski-lift to the top of Le Morond (1,419m) and skiing down past the CAF Chalet du Gros Morond into the slight valley to join the GTJ. Follow the GTJ westwards past the Chalet le Barthelette (possibility of overnight accommodation) to the popular ferme auberge La Boissaude (dortoirs), Rochejean, 25370 Les Hôpitaux Neufs. Tel: 81.39.17.35. Booking advised

The long summit ridge of Mont d'Or (1,464m) is one of the most attractive of the area and in good weather a diversion to the top is highly recommended. Its corniced rim above the steep east face is best seen at a safe distance. There is a very popular pisted trail from La Boissaude which rises past the Chalet La Cocquille to reach the open summit slopes. The easiest ascent is to go to the southern end of the ridge, where the CAF Cabane de Mont d'Or (open weekends) stands in a commanding position on a shelf overlooking the void. From here it is a short rise to the southernmost summit. You could of course traverse the whole of the undulating summit crest from Le Morond if you are not seeking overnight accommodation at Le Boissaude.

From the southern end of the crest regain the pisted trail which circles down to traverse past the farm of La Vermode. Leave the piste here to ski straight down the shallow valley to another large building. La Grande Echelle (dortoirs). The trail continues down the valley to enter Switzerland on the edge of the forest. The Swiss trails are marked with yellow ribbons tied to tree branches. Ski down the forest road to join another forest road in a deeper valley. Turn right here and in 2km reach a clearing with a tiny foresters' hut on the right. This is La Pisserette, a bivouac for backpackers. There is a very steep and narrow trail which ascends from La Piserette left to Muratte (1,220m), a farm on the plateau top of the hill, whence a more gentle descent is made to Les Charbonnières. A much easier ascent from La Pisserette is to continue up the main valley trail, with the Swiss border markers on the wall on the right, for another kilometre, where a more gentle track zig-zags left up the forest to the plateau top, to a fine descent. Join a snowploughed road but keep straight on to a final steep drop into the village of Les Charbonnières (Hotel, dortoirs), by the side of Lac Brenet. The shapely craggy peak of Dent de Vaulion (1,487m) lies

The foresters' Refuge de Pisserette lies in a small clearing.

across the lake, a guardian to the entrance of the Val de Joux, one of the most popular upland combes of the Jura, with innumerable skiing possibilities.

The trail continues across the road along the edge of the lake, which curls into a narrow causeway separating Lac Brenet from the much larger Lac de Joux. If the conditions are good you can continue to ski along the edge of the Lac de Joux - note the fine monument - to join the road at the far end of the village. Le Pont is a pleasant place with shops, hotels, dortoirs, youth hostel.

At the end of the village take the left fork road which rises towards a steep forested hillside with a long ski-lift. You can ride this lift if your technique is good, to the summit of Haut du Mollendruz (1,441m), a useful height gain. Alternatively follow the road towards the Col du Mollendruz from the base of the ski-tow for a short way to branch right up a shallow combe where a trail ascends through the forest to reach a low col west of Haut du Mollendruz. A slight descent leads to a broad flattish clearing at Prés de l'Haut. This point can be reached from the ski-lift summit by a sporting trail at first through dense trees and a steep descent onto a forest road which curls around the southern end the spur. Another steep drop leads to the clearing.

The clearing is a crossroad of trails, with the machined piste joining from the Col du Mollendruz on the left. Turn right, signed Col du Marchairuz. The trail follows a rising combe below the parallel crest of

Mont Tendre, past the long low farms of Le Maxel and Pré d'Etoy. A little further on the right is a tiny cabin. This is the Refuge Bon Acceuil, the most unusual refuge in the Jura, for it is a converted tramcar, complete with padded benches and cord luggage racks. My party of eight managed to spend a squashed night here in almost tropical heat, with a blizzard blowing outside!

The summit ridge of Mont Tendre is a worthy diversion from the main trail in clear weather. From Pré d'Etoy gain a shelf on the left, pass the Chalet de Pierre to a low col at the northernmost end of the switchback summit ridge. Follow this crest over the summit (1,679m) with the magnificent panorama of the Alps as companion. The snow on the ridge is often blown into elegant sastrugi, delightful to see but tricky to negotiate on skis, and it may be prudent to proceed on foot. Drop steeply to another col at the end of the summit ridge and either join the pisted trail along the combe on the right, or continue over the next forested humps. There is possibility of accommodation at the CAS Cabane Cunay or a little further at the Chalet Ski Club de Brassus. Pass the Monts de Biere to reach the road at the Col de Marchairuz (Hotel, dortoirs).

This point is reached more easily along the pisted trail which runs on the combes below the crest, almost level at first from the Bon Acceuil. At Grands Crosets Dessus bend left onto an upper shelf. Just past the Chalets des Combes is a long exhilarating descent, then walking again past the large farm of Pré de Denens to the summer road below the Col de Marchairuz.

If you want the trappings of civilization for the night turn left along the road and mount to the hotel. If bothies are your preference turn right along the well pisted road and follow it across the base of the upland combe. (Note the continuation of the trail along the Combe d'Amburnex.) The road leads towards Le Brassus, and after a kilometre, just below the highest point look for a minor trail which branches sharply left. This wends for a kilometre through dense woods, and where it starts to descend more steeply there is a dark wooden chalet on the left. This is the Chalet Inter Communale, an open refuge, with stove and wooden floored sleeping area upstairs. The Refuge de la Joratte, about 1½ kilometres further is tiny by comparison and theoretically you are not allowed to spend the night there except in emergency.

The main trail continues along the broad flat Combe des Amburnex. There is a short cut from the Col de Marchairuz. There is overnight accommodation at the Trois Chalets on the right. After passing the little knoll of Crêt de Grison, the trail twists through a gap to reach the

170

long low chalet Refuge les Pralets, another overnight stop.

An alternative trail from the Chalet Inter-Communale is straight ahead into a combe parallel to the Combe d'Amburnex. This is usually pisted and has more interesting skiing. There is more variety between clearing and forest, more undulations and fine views to Mont Sala. It joins the main trail just before Les Pralets.

Now the character changes. There are more ascents and descents, and interesting skiing. The trail mounts in forest under the slopes of Mont Pele before it swoops down to a large clearing at Le Vermeilley. Just before this note the trail going right, which offers a fine route to Le Cure over a col below the CAS Cabane du Carrox on the hill top. Thence a long descent is made to the pisted circuits around Le Cure.

The main trail however, continues from Le Vermeilley to Haut Mond and the road at La Givrine, on the Swiss side of the border. Note from Haut Mond it is a short ascent left, over the hill, to the CAS Cabane Rochefort, a fine refuge in a commanding position. A night here with sunset and sunrise views over the Alps is unforgettable. Like all the CAS huts in the Jura, if no-one is using them they are locked. If you are lucky enough to find them in use, you are welcome to stay the night.

The busy ski village of St. Cergue lies three kilometres down the road from La Givrine. (Full shopping facilities, plenty of accommodation, youth hostel.)

Just over the Col de la Givrine is the border village of La Cure, the terminus of the mountain railway which runs through St. Cergue to Nyon and main line rail connections.

LA GIVRINE to MENTHIÈRES
53.5km   3 days

Maps: D & R Sheet 34 Jura Sud. 1:50,000
Ski de Fond Massif du Jura. Sheets 5 and 6 1:25,000

		KM.	ACC.KM.
La Givrine	1,208m	0.00	0.00
Col de la Faucille	1,320m	20.50	20.50
Crêt de la Neige	1,717m	15.00	35.00
Refuge Pontouille	1,400m	12.00	47.00
Menthières	1,090m	6.00	53.00

171

No account is taken of extra distance involved in seeking accommodation at Lelex.

This is the most mountainous stage of the route which includes the highest summit of the Jura and a succession of shapely peaks. Good weather conditions are necessary for a safe passage, as the route can be very confusing in mist. The sharp ridge from Le Reculet to the Pierre de la Lune can be the crux of the expedition if the snow conditions are poor. The ridge can be heavily corniced, or it may be wind blown free of snow. If conditions are too bad on this section a descent to Lelex enables the neighbouring GTJ to be used to finish. The skier needs good control to safely traverse this section.

From the car park at La Givrine join a pisted trail which heads through a gap into the Vallon des Dappes, the extensive busy ski-lift area along the base of La Dôle. The whole flank of the mountain is networked with downhill ski pistes, perhaps the best of its type in the Jura, part of the large ski complex of Les Rousses/St. Cergue.

There are several possibilities from here:-

a)   The most elegant continuation is take a ski-lift to the summit of La Dôle (1,677m) and ski the crest south-west to reach Grand Sonnailley on the French frontier. Here join a ski piste system which is followed to La Vattay (Refuge) on the main road 3km below the Col da la Faucille. If you want to avoid the road there is a circuitous diversion from the Maison Forestière la Croix de Puthod, where a track runs south across steep forested slopes to a clearing at La Vesancière. A little further join a forest road which zig-zags in and out of little combes to join the main road 1km before the Col de la Faucille.

b)   From La Tabagnoz, at the end of the Vallon des Dappes, a pisted trail wends around a spur of La Dôle to Grand Sonnailley.

c)   From La Tabagnoz continue straight down the attractive valley to join ski pistes along the floor of the long combe to Mijoux (Shops, hotels, gîte). The telesiege can then be used to reach the Col de la Faucille. This route is useful in poor weather.

The Col de la Faucille is a major road pass over the Jura. A road just below the summit of the pass leads past large car parks to the main ski station. There are hotels, restaurants and a hive of activity.

The continuation of the forest road past the base of the ski installations is used as an easy downhill piste. Ascend the side of this with care - you are certain to be against the main flow of traffic. The 'road' zig-zags up to another set of ski-lifts, where an unpisted continuation

172

The deserted upland farms are almost buried by snow. This one lies above the Col de la Faucille on the approach to the Crête.

of the road goes horizontally right. Follow this away from the crowds to rise past the isolated farm of Le Crozat below the first of several cols on the crest to the left. The steep peak above the col, Montrond (1,596m) can be climbed and the ridge followed along its undulations, taking care with steep descents. A much easier route is to traverse the western flank of the mountain well above the tree line and above several chalets. The fine dome ahead crowned by a huge metal cross, is the Colomby de Gex (1,680m), a worthwhile objective. Bypass the next summit as it has a steep descent at the far side, to gain easier slopes and the Col de Crozet. Descend across the downhill ski pistes and ski-lifts to round the steep cone of Montoisey. This area above Lelex vies with Les Rousses as the best downhill ski resort in the Jura. Its pistes link with those on the Swiss side and you are certain to meet many people.

The Lelex area makes a convenient overnight break, thus leaving a full day to spend on the intricacies and delights of the following final stage of the route.

A little further than the telecabin top station and almost at the same level - follow the telephone poles - is the Chalet la Loge which may be open for accommodation. (A trail runs 2km along a shelf to Brulat d'en Haut, shown on the ski map as an open unguarded refuge but likely to be locked.) From La Loge a steep descent of the ski piste drops to the next shelf which hosts a fine CAF Refuge le Ratou,

173

On the Crête, heading for Colomby de Gex.

another overnight possibility. A careful descent of the continuing very steep downhill piste leads to the busy ski village of Lelex. Where the trail joins the road, opposite the post office is a gîte d'étape (M. S/C). Other accommodation is available in the village. (Shops, tourist information).

If you decide that the descent of steep, difficult downhill pistes on cross-country skis is foolhardy, then the telecabin gives a swift ride to Lelex, painless except on the pocket.

To continue the traverse ascend by telecabin from Lelex (600m ascent). From the station ski right, signed Crêt de la Neige, and follow the edge of a piste which curls below the cone of Montoisey to the col at its south. Here the bustle of downhill ski is left behind as steep slopes are zig-zagged to the plateau top of the Grand Crêt (1,702m). For the rest of the day the skiing is the best the Jura can offer, over an isolated mountain range of some complexity which requires good weather and good snow conditions for a safe passage.

At first the Grand Crêt is tame enough, as it drops to a slight col where a huge doline is avoided. The ensuing plateau of the Crêt de la Neige is quite unlike any other summit in the Jura, for it is a craggy plateau dotted with tiny trees and riven into parallel ridges and ravines. The main ravine is narrow and deep - and it splits the full length of the summit ridge, heading straight towards the shapely cone of Le Reculet. It is possible to by-pass the summit by using this ravine but you will surely want to bag this delectable high point. Its height seems to vary according to which map you are using, between 1,717m and 1,723m, but it is certainly marginally higher than its neighbour, Le Reculet.

To reach the summit, follow the rocky crest to the right of the main ravine. Rock steps have to be negotiated and a chasm avoided (a cave here could be useful shelter). The top is surmounted by a rickety timber triangulation structure. There is talk of its replacement with something more grand. The short descent on its far side is rocky and steep. Skis may need to be taken off hereabouts.

Easier skiing continues over undulating terrain to mount the steep cone of Le Reculet, with its huge cross. The views are more extensive here and by now the Alpine giants across the plain should be familiar companions.

The next section of the traverse lies above the impressive deep cirque of Roche Franche on a ridge which becomes very narrow and airy. Snow conditions may necessitate a traverse on the east flank to avoid any danger of cornices. After heavy snowfall there could be avalanche risk. In icy conditions the traverse could be unpleasant. Hopefully you will encounter good snow and little difficulty. At the other extreme, the crest may be windblown and bare, which will necessitate taking skis off to walk. The end of the ridge is marked by a conical peak, the Pierre de la Lune, below which in a clearing is the Chalet du Gralet, a backpackers' refuge in a fine situation at the top edge of the forest.

The route is easier but not straightforward as it winds in and out of indentations on the tree clad eastern flank of the now almost horizontal crest. Another clearing is reached with the Refuge Pontouille in its centre, a fine overnight stop for backpackers. The trail descends intricately through the forest to round a steep shoulder where the ski pistes of Menthières are joined on a flat shelf.

Keep right on the edge of the forested shelf to join a forest road right. This curves around the head of a valley and descends to Menthières a tiny ski centre, with a welcoming Centre Sportif Montagnard (dortoirs).

If you have time and inclination before descending to Menthières continue to the Col du Sac to reach the final summit of the Jura, the Grand Crêt d'Eau 1,612m, a worthy finale.

From Menthières a road drops down to Confort and the town of Bellegarde. (TGV).

Bad Weather Route from Lelex

In poor weather or conditions of very deep soft snow, the high route along the crest from Lelex to Menthières is inadvisable. In this case it is best to join the GTJ to finish the traverse at Giron.

From Lelex follow the valley trail for 1.5km up the combe towards Mijoux. At Septfontaines cross the river left and follow a track which ascends steeply past La Pralouse to join the GTJ near the head of Bellecombe.

CIRCUIT OF THE VAL DE JOUX

87km   5 days

Maps: Carte National de la Suisse. 1:25,000 Sheets 1240 Les
Rousses, 1241 Marchairuz, 1221 Le Sentier, 1201 Mouthe.
These are finely detailed and cover all the area except one
small corner at Le Pont.
Alternatively the K & F Carte Speciale du Jura. 1:50,000
Sheet 6 Vallee de Joux covers the area except a small corner
near Les Rousses!
The D & R Au Coeur du Jura; 1:50,000 Sheet 33, fills the
gap and is a useful addition.

Between Vallorbe in Switzerland and Les Rousses in France, lies one
of the most attractive areas of the Jura for safe winter ski touring. The
Val de Joux is a broad flat upland combe, with small villages scattered
along its length of 30 kilometres from Le Pont to Les Rousses. To the
south-east of the valley is a wide and varied plateau edged by Mont
Tendre (1,679m), the highest summit of the Central Jura. On the
other side of the valley is the much more densely forested, lower crest
of Risoux, which is crossed by the GTJ.

Vallorbe lies on a main TGV rail line (Dijon-Lausanne), with a
characterful mountain rail link up the gorge to Le Pont and Le
Brassus. Les Rousses at the other end of the valley is also close to a
unique little mountain railway which runs from Nyon, on the shore of
Lake Geneva, to La Cure, only 2.5km from Les Rousses. Perhaps the
greatest attraction of a circuit is for car based skiers. Note that after a
heavy snowfall, chains may be required. Also beware of high
ambitions as heavy trail breaking may require a change of plan to a
shortened circuit. The base of the Val de Joux lies at around 1,000m,
the surrounding crests are between 1,200m and 1,500m. Its height
and position generally ensure a good snow coverage during the prime
ski months, when the possibilities of a circular tour are legion. The
most obvious tour uses the GTJ from Les Rousses to Metabief, then
the TJS/Crest route for the return over Mont d'Or and the Combe
d'Amburnex. The bulk of this is described in previous chapters, and

The Chalet Inter-Communale near Marchairuz. The stove generated so much heat that half the roof avalanched!

it matters little which way it is traversed.

A shorter traverse, which includes more off-piste and semi-piste is along the crest of the Grand and Petit Risoux. This offers an attractive option if you like to use map reading skills, for the dense forest is a challenge with its maze of forest roads used as ski trails. The route lies in and out of the frontier, confusing at times, but Switzerland can be recognised by yellow signposts and yellow marker ribbons in the trees!

Le Pont to Marchairuz   18km

This is briefly described in the Traverse of the Crêtes (see pages 168 to 171), but a few additional comments may be useful.

1.   Novices should treat the ski-lift to Haut du Mollendruz with caution, for even experienced cross-country skiers find it a difficult ride with a rucksack.

2.   There is an alternative pisted trail which runs parallel to the main trail below the crest of Mont Tendre. This trail is more varied over a complex area of small hillocks in clearings and forest. There is a small backpackers' shelter, the Refuge du Bois a Ban. Pass the Chalet du Grand Essert and Les Chaumilles to join the main trail at La Rolat on the road below the Col du Marchairuz.

3.   If snow conditions render a full traverse too arduous, then a shortened version is achieved by descending the pisted road to Le Brassus. The road descends in gentle bends to a final steeper drop.

The ski trail skirts the edge of frozen Lac de Joux at Le Pont.

Before the final descent it is possible to join downhill ski pistes on the right - if your technique is up to it! Walk through the village and pass a gap on the other side of the flat valley floor, to reach the start of the pisted ski trails from La Thomassette. A choice of route ensues into the heights of the Grand Risoux, one of which passes the Chalet Capt, an open foresters' cabin of great character, to join the trail along the crest of the Risoux.

Marchairuz to Les Rousses   25km

On the main trail of the TJS/Crêtes Route just before Le Vermeilley (see page 171) take the lesser track right to Le Cure, by way of L'Arxière. This lies at the head of a long valley bounded on the north by Le Noirmont (1,567m) and smaller hills to the south, one of which is topped by the CAS Cabane du Carrox. The long valley gives an exhilarating descent past Les Coppettes to join the well pisted trails at its base and reach the small frontier village of Le Cure. (There is a large car park almost under the nose of the customs post, a good spot to leave a vehicle for several days.) Cross the railway and turn right along the main road which soon bears left. Keep straight on along a minor road which serves as a ski piste into Les Rousses.

Les Rousses is a ski centre throbbing with activity - shops, traffic, people. It has every facility and plenty of accommodation. Don't try

178

to ski through the town or the *gendarmes* will pounce. The dedicated backpacker will stock-up at the shops and head for the quieter parts of the Forêt de Risoux which offer spartan bothy accommodation and a gîte d'étape.

LES ROUSSES to LE PONT
44km   2 days

Les Rousses	0.00	0.00
Chalet Rose	7.00	7.00
Chalet Gaillard	6.00	13.00
Chalet Capt	6.00	19.00
La Grande Landoz	5.00	24.00
Refuge du Poteau	10.00	34.00
La Pisserette	4.00	38.00
Les Charbonnières	4.00	42.00
Le Pont	2.00	44.00

From the lower square of Les Rousses a short steep descent cuts across to the road at Les Rousses en Bas. Turn right along the road 300m to a forest road left at the entrance to the Forêt du Risoux. This is the start of the ski de fond trails and a notice board map displays the trails. The permutations are many and the route described is a recommendation only. If there has been a heavy snowfall you will need to use any of the trails which are pisted. Every junction is well signed and the whole area is justly popular. The forested plateau is a broad complex mix of combe and hillock which gives good undulating skiing and needs careful map reading to keep track of progress.

The forest road rises steeply onto the plateau and after semi-circling a little combe take a fork right signed Chalet Rose along the Route de la Combette aux Quilles. Keep right again at another fork and in another 3km reach the Chalet Rose, a large foresters' chalet which is a useful backpackers' stop, although the sleeping area upstairs is cold and draughty. (7km from Les Rousses.)

A trail does continue along the Combette but a more interesting route is to fork left at the Chalet Rose to join a parallel trail at La Croix du Tronc. Turn right here and continue to another major trail junction at the Chalet des Ministres (1,227m), another possible backpackers' shelter.

Turn right along the GTJ, which seems very busy compared with the other trails, to another junction at Plan des Buchaillers. Keep right, still on the GTJ, for another km to a left fork at a bend. If you come to a broad clearing on your left you have overshot. The left fork is signed to the Chalet Flacan, (Chalet Gaillard), a popular gîte d'étape which offers meals or self cooking facilities. It lies at the base of a low hill not far from the Swiss frontier, (13km from Les Rousses).

The next problem is to cross the frontier and make the link with the Swiss trails on the other side. You may have to do some careful navigation along unpisted trails. Take a trail more or less north from the gîte. One trail goes straight to the Roche Bernard, overlooking the steep plateau edge and the flat combe of Chapelle-des-Bois, but fork right from this trail to cross the frontier at a gap in the hill. Continue more or less at the same level to join the top of a forest road just above the Refuge des Italiens, (possibility of shelter). You should have joined the Swiss piste system which radiates from La Thomassette, but there is no guarantee that all the trails will be pisted. There is a possible route more or less at the same level, or easier, a descent to the clearing of Pré Derrière. Take the left fork just before the farm and rise to a right branch which leads to join another trail just above the Chalet Capt. This is a large foresters' chalet in a small clearing. It is left open in winter and can provide an excellent overnight stop for backpackers.

We have joined a recognised ski route along the crest of the Grand Risoux, which should carry yellow marker ribbons in the trees and if you are lucky will be tracked but unpisted. Above the Chalet Capt the trail goes right and stays on the Swiss side of the crest making use of the maze of summer paths which are difficult to follow if the snow is untracked. At the top edge of a clearing, on the French side of the crest is Grande Landoz (1,377m) (Restaurant, possibility of overnight). The route continues more or less on the crest, although the dense forest limits the views. The trail lies on the Swiss side of the frontier, past the open refuge of Les Mines, another possibility for backpackers, to cross a forest road, the Chemin Chez la Tante. After a further 2.5km a track descends right to the clearing of Grande Tepe, and the gîte of Le Levant, which offers accommodation. This is on the piste system which radiates from Le Lieu in the valley and could be useful in poor conditions. However, the direct route keeps along the trail passing between Grand Crêt (1,419m) and another lesser knoll to a pleasant descent to the edge of a clearing above Les Plainox. Climb gently to the Crêt Charbonnet whence another descent leads to a snow-ploughed road.

Les Charbonnières lies a few kilometres right down the road, but the ski route takes a more devious but quite beautiful alternative. At the head of the road col stands a bare but large shelter, the Refuge du Poteau, without a stove and used mainly by day excursionists. At the side of the refuge a trail along the Chemin de la Grande Combe gives a long very gentle descent where you can just stand on your skis and glide gracefully for just over two kilometres to where a steep forest road branches off on the right. (Backpackers could go another kilometre down the main valley trail to the foresters' cabin of La Pisserette in a small clearing, an idyllic overnight stop.)

The forest road winds steeply up the hill to a clearing on its flat crest, then gives a long gentle run down to Les Charbonnières. Where the first snow-ploughed road is joined at a farm, keep right, cross another road, and take a short cut down to the village. (Hotel, dortoir.) Through the square go to the edge of the Lac Brenet, a beautiful sight especially if its edge is laced with ice, with the bold cliffs of the Dent de Vaulion behind. The trail runs along the edge of the lake, to join the road for a very short distance along the causeway, then the edge of the much larger Lac de Joux can be followed to complete the circuit at Le Pont.

If you have time to spare, **Mont d'Or** (1,463m) is a very highly recommended extension to the circuit. Continue from the Pisserette down the Grande Combe for another 2 kilometres to a forest road junction left. This winds up a side valley to emerge from the forest at the frontier and join a GTJ liaison trail which ascends gently up a broad combe. Past the Chalet of La Petite Echelle to another much larger chalet, the Grande Echelle (dortoirs). At La Vermode Chalet further up the combe join the pisted ski trail which winds right to the edge of the Mont d'Or escarpment. There is a CAF cabin open weekends on a flat shoulder with commanding views. The summit of the mountain is easily gained along the crest of the ridge, but beware of the huge cornices. If the snow is good you can make a sporting direct descent to La Vermode to regain the ascent route.

USEFUL ADDRESSES

Literature is available from the following. It is worth writing to each of the three départmental tourist offices as each publish their own leaflets and do not stray into neighbouring territory. Ask for literature about the GTJ. Useful leaflets cover the accommodation.

Comité Départemental du Tourisme Jurassien
Prefecture - 55, rue Saint-Désiré
39021 LONS-LE-SAUNIER
France.
This includes the central section of the Jura - La Pesse, Lajoux, Les Rousses.

Comité Départemental du Tourisme de l'Ain
34, Rue Général Delestraint
B.P. 78
01002 BOURG-EN-BRESSE Cedex
France.
Similar to the above but covers the Dept. of Ain and the southern section of the Jura and Bugey - Mijoux, Lelex, Giron, Menthières.

Association Départementale du Tourisme du Doubs
Hôtel du Département
25031 BESANCON Cedex
France.
Covers the northern area of the French Jura, including Mouthe, Metabief and Les Fourgs.

Bureaux des Gîtes
Étapes Jura
LAJOUX
39310 SEPTMONCEL
France.
This is the organisation which will book a sequence of consecutive gîtes for the GTJ. They also publish a most useful leaflet which lists all the gîtes along the GTJ.

If you do not get what you want from the above, you could write to the various individual resorts:
Syndicat d'Initiative, 39220 LES ROUSSES, Jura, France
Syndicat d'Initiative, LES FOURGS, Doubs, France
Syndicat d'Initiative, METABIEF, Doubs, France

Tourist information on the Swiss Jura can be obtained from the following:

Lac de Joux-Mont Tendre area -
   Office du Tourisme de la Vallée de Joux, Hotel de Ville,
   1347 Le Sentier, Switzerland.

The half buried Chalet Capt, entered through a dug-out hole.

Chasseron-Creux du Van-Mont Racine area -
    Office Neuchâtelois du Tourisme
    Rue de Trésor 9 (place des Halles)
    CH-200 Neuchâtel, Switzerland.

Guided Tours
École Jurassienne de Raid, Chapelle-des-Bois, 25240 Mouthe, France.
An organisation which offers guided ski tours in the Jura, as well as courses for novices (in French). Included are 2 week trips on the traverse of the crêtes, more or less as described in this book.

Raid Jura, École de Ski des Rousses, Premanon 39220 Les Rousses, France.
Guided ski tours available for 1 week along the GTJ and circuit of Val de Joux.

L'Union Départementale des Centres-École et Foyers de ski de fond
63 rue Hoche
01200 BELLEGARDE-SUR-VALSERINE
France.
Information on the ski centres at Giron and Menthières. Guided tours of a week are organised by these centres, including the GTJ from Mont d'Or to Giron and the Crêtes from Lac de Joux to Menthières.

Waymark Holidays, 295 Lillie Road, London SW6 7LL.
British specialists in cross-country ski holidays. The Jura is one of a number of continental venues.

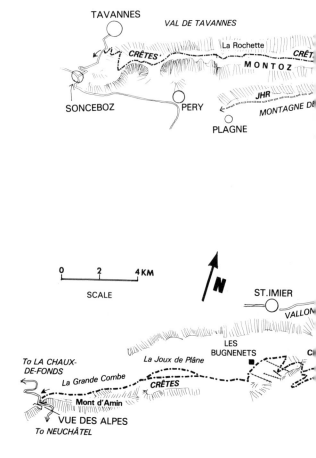

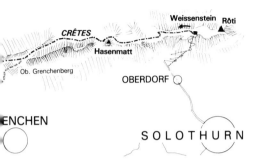

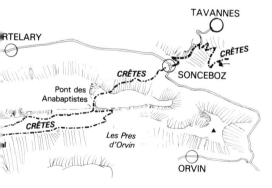

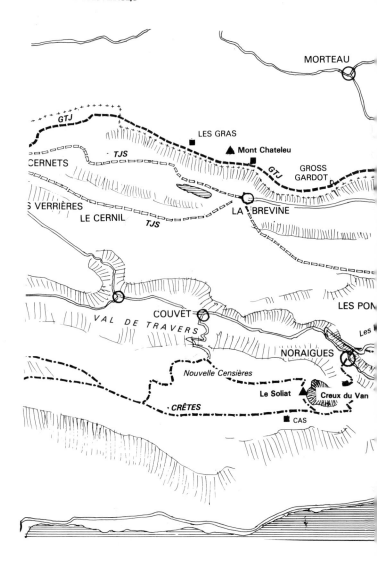

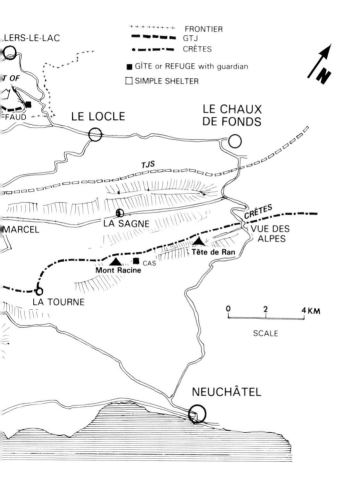

FRONTIER
GTJ
CRÊTES
■ GÎTE or REFUGE with guardian
☐ SIMPLE SHELTER

LERS-LE-LAC

T OF

FAUD

LE LOCLE

LE CHAUX
DE FONDS

TJS

MARCEL

LA SAGNE

CRÊTES

VUE DES
ALPES

Tête de Ran

CAS

Mont Racine

LA TOURNE

0   2   4 KM

SCALE

NEUCHÂTEL

187

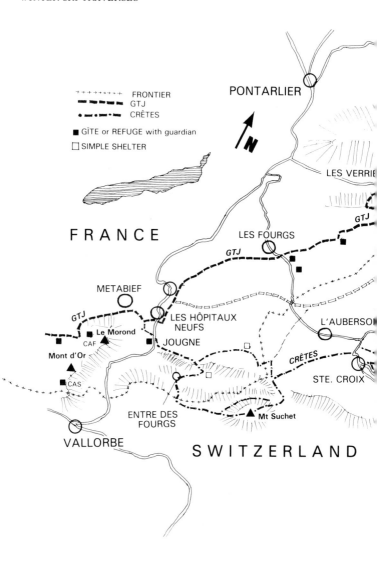

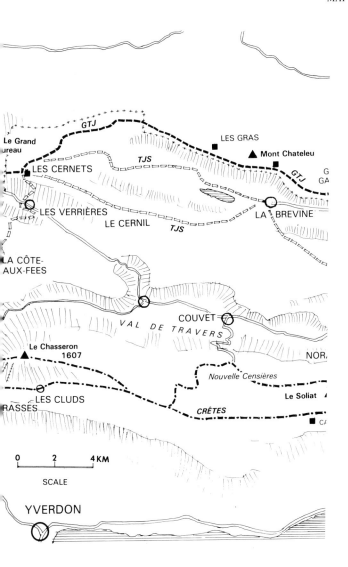

Le Grand
ureau

GTJ

LES GRAS

▲ Mont Chateleu

LES CERNETS

TJS

G
GA

GTJ

LES VERRIÈRES

LE CERNIL

TJS

LA BREVINE

LA CÔTE-
AUX-FEES

VAL DE TRAVERS

COUVET

▲ Le Chasseron
1607

NOR

Nouvelle Censières

LES CLUDS

RASSES

Le Soliat

CRÊTES

C

0   2   4 KM

SCALE

YVERDON

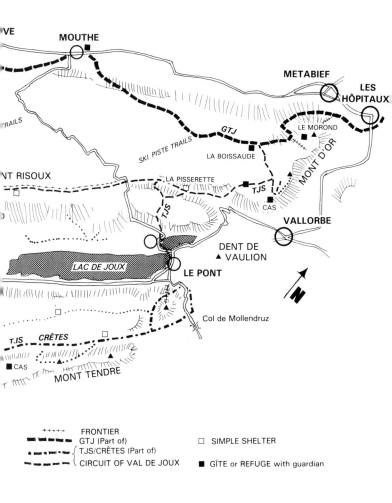

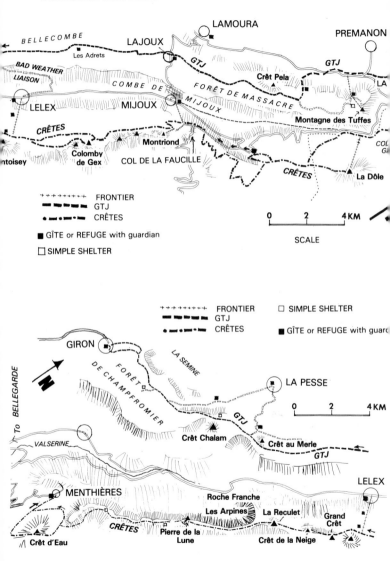

FRONTIER
GTJ
CRÊTES

■ GÎTE or REFUGE with guardian

□ SIMPLE SHELTER

0   2   4 KM

SCALE

FRONTIER   □ SIMPLE SHELTER
GTJ
CRÊTES   ■ GÎTE or REFUGE with guard

0   2   4 KM